The Satellite Atlas

David Flint

 Belitha Press

First published in the UK by Belitha Press Limited
31 Newington Green, London N16 9PU
Copyright in this format © Belitha Press 1995
Text copyright © David Flint 1995
Illustrations copyright © Belitha Press 1995
Cartography copyright © Terry Allen and
Nick Skelton 1995

Designer: Guy Callaby
Picture researcher: Juliet Duff
Editor: Maria O'Neill
Consultant: Steve Watts

ISBN 1 85561 394 8 (hardback)
ISBN 1 85561 519 3 (paperback)

Picture acknowledgements: Bruce Coleman Ltd : 58 top.
Geospace: 33 inset. Robert Harding Picture Library: 10 top
right and bottom, 22 both, 24, 29 top Spot Image, 32,
34 centre right, 36 centre, 40 bottom, 42 bottom, 46
bottom, 48 both, 50, 54 both. The Hutchison Library:
16, 34 centre left, 38 both. Magnum Photos: 26 centre
Abbas, 30 centre Bruno Barbey, 36 bottom Jean Gaumy.
NASA: title page, contents page, 6 top, 13 inset, 25 inset,
31 top and bottom right, 35, 39 top, 41 inset, 43 both,
45 inset, 49 top, 53 inset, 59 top, 60 top, 62-3 bottom.
NPA Group: 55 bottom left. Science Photo Library: 4 both,
57, 61 bottom Tom Van Sant/Geosphere Project, Santa
Monica, 5, 6 bottom, 9 top inset, 11 both, 13, 15, 17
bottom left, 29 bottom, 31 bottom left, 33, 37 inset, 45,
47, 49 bottom right, 53, 55 top and bottom right Earth
Satellite Corporation, 5, 9 centre inset, 57 inset NASA, 9,
17 top and bottom right Worldsat International, 10 top
left Alex Bartel, 15 inset, 21 inset, 35 inset, 61 top NRSC
Ltd, 19 both, 23 inset, 37, 41, 47 inset Geospace, 44 right
Simon Fraser, 49 bottom left, 51 all RETSEC, Japan, 59
bottom David Baum and David Angus, 60 bottom Doug
Allan. Frank Spooner Pictures: 7 top, 18 bottom, 20
bottom, 26 bottom, 42 centre, 46 top, 52 centre. Still
Pictures: 12 Julio Etchart/Reportage, 14 centre, 28 centre
Mark Edwards 14 bottom Sonja Iskov/2 Maj, 18 centre and
44 left Jorgen Schytte, 21, 23, 25, 27 and 39 DRA, 26 top
Jecko Vassilev, 28 bottom Hjalte Tim, 30 bottom Romano
Cagnoni, 40 centre Oliver Gillie, 52 bottom Paul Harrison.
Tony Stone Images: 8. Zefa: 20 centre, 34 bottom,
56 both, 58 bottom. Front Cover: Tom Van Sant/
Geosphere Project, Santa Monica/Science Photo Library.

Printed in Singapore for Imago

Satellite keys throughout this atlas are used to
provide indicators of land use or natural features.
The colours are approximate and may vary from
place to place.

Words in **bold** are explained in the glossary on
page 62.

Contents

Introduction

When people want a really good view of an object or a place they go up high to look down on it. The countries of the world have very different and complex landscapes. In the past, aircraft took aerial photographs of these landscapes and places such as cities or forests to capture the view from above. Now satellites out in space can provide views of even larger areas of the Earth's surface.

Different types of satellite

This atlas uses images from different satellites. Some were taken on space shuttle missions. Others come from weather satellites which are so high in space that they can view most of one side of the Earth at one time. Other images come from satellites closer

to the Earth, usually about 705 km up. These give more detailed images and are close enough to show the layout of streets in cities, or rivers and lakes in rural areas.

Remote sensing

All satellites are like platforms in space with different instruments which observe and record images of the Earth and then send them back down to us. This process is called remote sensing.

▼ This image of the Earth is one that most people know. It is made up of thousands of separate images recorded by weather satellites. The images were compiled into a vast database using a super computer which created this composite image.

▼ This is another composite image of the Earth. It shows a different view of the world centred on the Western Pacific. The Pacific is one of the fastest developing parts of the world. Many of the countries around the Pacific are becoming more important as their economies develop.

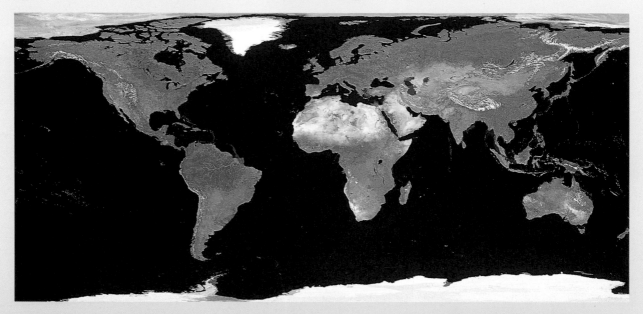

A satellite's orbit

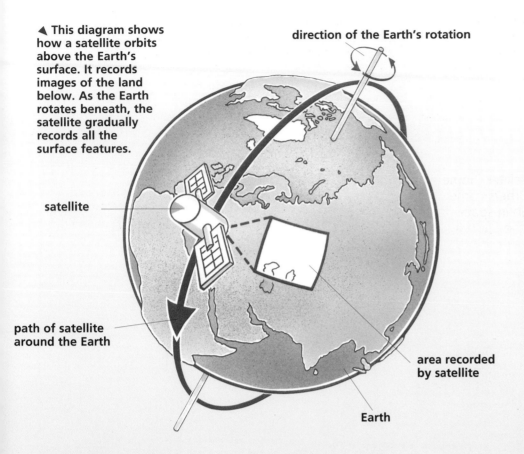

◄ This diagram shows how a satellite orbits above the Earth's surface. It records images of the land below. As the Earth rotates beneath, the satellite gradually records all the surface features.

direction of the Earth's rotation

satellite

path of satellite around the Earth

area recorded by satellite

Earth

Satellites in space
Most satellites are launched into space by rockets which take them to the correct height. Then they start orbiting the Earth. The satellites can travel at great speed and use very little energy once they are in space. Some orbit the Earth 20 or more times every day.

Many satellites follow a polar orbit, which means they pass over both North and South Poles. They repeat this orbit over and over again. As the Earth rotates on its axis below, the satellites eventually record the whole surface.

A changing world
Most satellites stay up for several years. Some satellites record many images of particular parts of the world at different times. These images can then be compared to see changes which occur from one year to the next or the changes caused by a natural or man-made disaster.

Invisible light
People only see the **visible spectrum** of light from red to violet. This is only part of the whole **electromagnetic spectrum**, which ranges from gamma and X-rays on short wavelengths through to infra-red, micro waves and radio waves on long wavelengths. Satellites have sensors to allow them to see all parts of the spectrum. Once the pictures have been processed by computer, people can see them as well.

► The US space shuttle blasts off from Cape Canaveral, USA, on another mission. Some of the images used in this atlas have been taken by cameras on board the space shuttle.

Satellites at work

The sensors on satellites detect the **radiation** that is given off from everything on the Earth's surface. Most satellites measure the radiation coming from areas 30 x 30 metres in lots of little squares called pixels. Later the data from the pixels is put together to give one complete image.

Ground receiving stations
The radiation from each pixel is changed into numbers (digital data) which are stored on magnetic tape on the satellite. Data is then sent to a ground receiving station in signals like radio waves.

These two satellite images show the difference between natural light and artificial colour. The image of Kuwait City (right) shows the pattern of main roads in natural light, as well as the layout of the city. In the image below of north-east USA and Canada, the colours have been strengthened to show the lakes, forest and tundra more clearly.

Computer-generated images
Once the data is stored on magnetic tape in ground stations, it passes into a special computer which generates images. These images can be altered to show natural colours, or just to show infra-red. The computer image is converted into photographs which make them easier to look at and use.

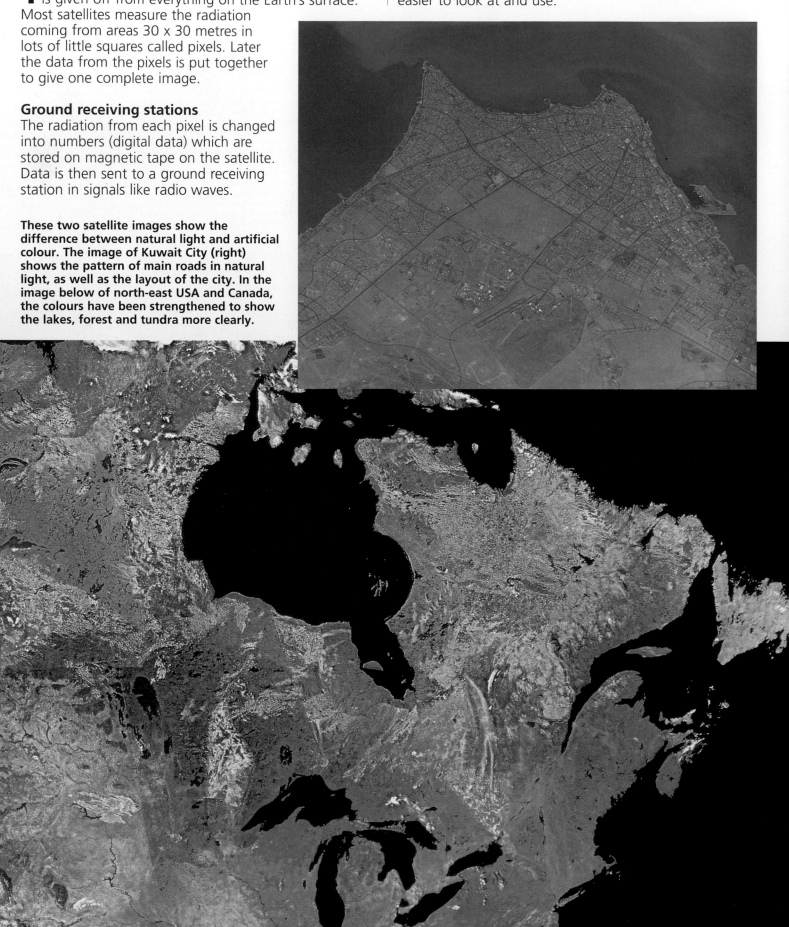

Who uses satellite images?

Many countries use satellite images, especially countries which are now undergoing **economic development**. The images show rivers, roads and settlements and are used to make maps, especially of remote areas.

Shape of the land

Ordinary photographs do not show the **geology** of the Earth. Satellites see all the different parts of the electromagnetic spectrum, which means they can identify different types of rock. Oil companies use satellite images when they are deciding where to drill for oil, and geologists use them when trying to predict a volcanic eruption. Some images are used to check the changing shapes of sandbanks so that ships can be warned and accidents avoided. Satellites can also track the movement of hurricanes and icebergs.

▲ **Satellites allow journalists to broadcast news all round the world within minutes. Wherever they are in the world, journalists like the one above in the Gulf can send their reports via satellite links. The umbrella dish sends the signals to a satellite which transmits them to other countries.**

How to use this atlas

- The main text in each section gives information on that part of the world.
- The boxes at the top of the page contain information on the people who live there, the environment and the major political concerns of the region.
- A small locator map at the beginning of each section looks at where in the world the area is found.
- Two or more satellite images are shown for each area. These images give a different view of the world from conventional maps.
- Keys are used to explain the colours in many of the images.
- An ordinary map shows how the area looks in most atlases.
- Captions describe each image in detail and explain its colours and important features.

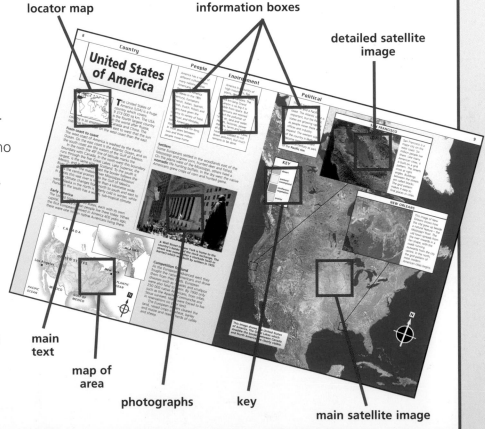

locator map

information boxes

detailed satellite image

main text

map of area

photographs

key

main satellite image

United States of America

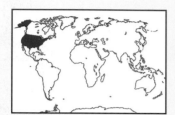

The United States of America (USA) is a huge country which covers 9 373 000 sq km. The USA is the fourth largest country in the world after Russia, Canada and China. The country is so enormous from east to west that the sun rises five hours later on the west coast than the east.

From coast to coast
The west coast of America is washed by the Pacific Ocean. On the east coast is the Atlantic Ocean, and on the south coast are the waters of the Gulf of Mexico.

In the north the 49° line of latitude marks the boundary with Canada. In the north-west this boundary runs through the five Great Lakes. Lake Superior, the largest, is the same size as Scotland. To the south is Mexico, and in the south-east the border follows the River Grande. The massive river Mississippi-Missouri drains the central prairies into the Gulf of Mexico. In places this vast river is more than a kilometre wide.

The climate changes from north to south and east to west. Alaska in the north is bitterly cold in winter, while Florida in the south has a warm, sub-tropical climate.

Early America
The United States has 50 states, each with its own capital, and 249 million people live there today. When the first Europeans arrived in America 400 years ago, there were one million native Americans living there.

America has a range of different cultures from many nations. Native Americans, black Africans (brought to America as slaves in the 18th century), Europeans (French, Italian, Spanish, British, Dutch, Polish) and Asians have given the country its variety of food, art, music and lifestyles. Some Americans never stay in one place for long. In most years between two and three million people move home.

America is a country of high mountains, flat plains, deserts, salt lakes and deep canyons. The 349 km long Grand Canyon is so big it is visible from space. But Americans are worried about the pollution of their air, land and water. Homes, factories, power stations, farms and traffic all play a part in this. Laws have been passed to cut down pollution, but much remains to be done.

Settlers
Some Europeans settled in the woodlands east of the Mississippi and grew corn, hunted deer and fished. On the plains west of the Mississippi, others lived a **nomadic** life hunting buffalo. In the dry west the native Americans grew crops of corn and hunted game.

▲ **Wall Street in New York is home to the country's banks and the stock exchange. The street was named after a stockade (wall or barrier) which was built by settlers in 1653.**

Competition for land
As the Europeans advanced west they fought the native Americans and drove them from their lands. European diseases such as measles and smallpox were also fatal to them. By 1900 only 250 000 native Americans, from tribes such as the Apache, Commanche and Sioux survived. Many were forced to live in reservations on poor land.

The European settlers cleared the land, raised crops of wheat, barley and maize and reared herds of cattle and sheep.

CANADA

ALASKA

UNITED STATES

New York

Los Angeles

ATLANTIC OCEAN

MEXICO

GULF OF MEXICO

PACIFIC OCEAN

N

The US has both an Atlantic and a Pacific coast. The Atlantic coast is important, but the Pacific states are growing rapidly as people move there and offices and industry expand. The western side of the country is likely to become more important in the 21st century as part of the **Pacific rim**.

SAN FRANCISCO

San Francisco is a major city on the west coast. Six million people live there. Like many American cities, it is built on a grid pattern. The streets cross at right angles. Buildings between the streets are called blocks. The grid pattern makes it easy to find places in cities.

KEY

	mountains
	grassland
	forest
	sea

NEW ORLEANS

This image of New Orleans shows how the city grew up beside a natural feature – the Mississippi River. The old town spreads from the river inwards in a fan shape, with the roads running outwards from the city centre. In the north, the grid pattern of most modern American cities begins.

N

This is the United States of America. The Great Lakes which straddle the border between Canada and North America are clearly visible.

United States of America

The USA is a rich, powerful country in which three-quarters of the people live in towns and cities. City centres are dominated by tall office blocks and shops. These are surrounded by industrial areas and **residential suburbs.** Towns spread along main roads with hypermarkets and offices on the edge of built-up areas.

▲ An oil well off the coast of the Gulf of Mexico. Oil is vital to America's wealth.

◄ A combine harvester cuts and threshes in a wheatfield.

Cities and industry
Some cities, such as Los Angeles, have grown up from a series of different town centres to form one huge, sprawling, urban area connected by 800 km of freeway. American cities suffer from a great many traffic jams, especially at rush hours, as well as smog and rising crime rates.

Cities are also centres of industry, which have created much of the country's wealth. Many large industrial cities are in the north and east. Products made there range from steel, cars and textiles, to washing machines, paint and medicines.

Moving south
Recently many new factories have been opened in the south and west, especially in Texas, California and Arizona. Here there are huge areas of land, a large labour force, lower wages, growing markets and warm climates. Thousands of people have left the old steel-based industries of the north and east to work in the

new petro-chemical, micro-electronics and aerospace industries of the south and west. As the new cities expanded they provided jobs in services: shops, offices, and transport.

A wealth of food
Two-thirds of the USA is farmland where crops such as wheat, barley, maize, cotton, rice and tobacco are grown. Cattle, sheep and pigs are reared and in Florida and California, fruit and vegetables are grown.

Larger farms
American farms are becoming bigger. They have grown from an average 85 hectares in 1950 to 190 hectares in 1990. Only large farms can afford the high costs of machinery, irrigation, labour, chemicals such as fertilizers and borrowing. These are essential to modern **intensive farming**.

▼ A native American woman from the Navajo tribe, the largest group of native people in America. The Navajo are famous for their crafts especially, silversmithing and weaving.

DID YOU KNOW?

● America is the biggest producer in the world of beef, beer, cheese, chickens, grapefruit, maize, paper, strawberries and tomatoes.

● America is the second biggest producer (after China) of coal, cotton, pork and tobacco, the second biggest producer (after South Africa) of gold, and the second biggest producer of cars (after Japan).

Farm and food workers
Farms today are large and **mechanized** so they employ fewer and fewer people (14 million in 1950; 2.7 million in 1993). Two million farms produce America's food. Most of these are family farms, but large companies are becoming more important.

Twenty million people are needed to store, process, transport and market all this food. Ten thousand different products pour into hypermarkets, processed, labelled and packaged. The USA is the world's largest exporter of food. Sixty per cent of the food is grain, which goes mainly to Europe, Asia and Africa.

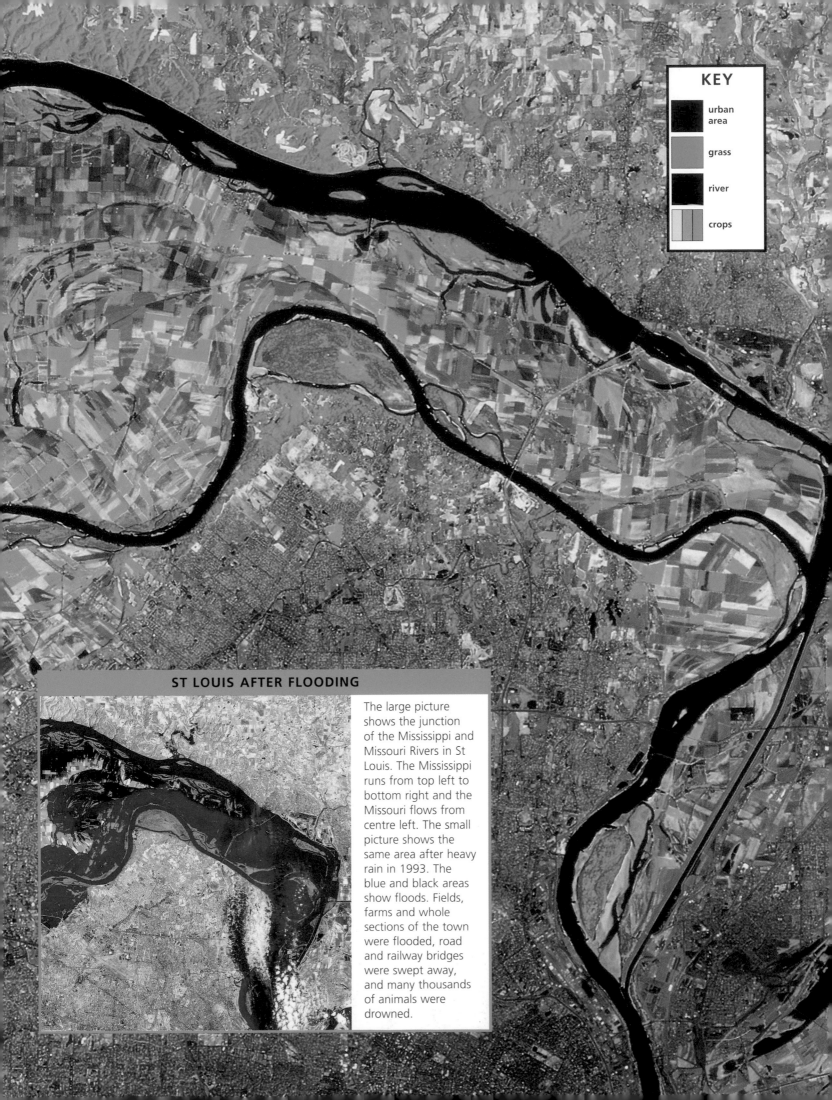

ST LOUIS AFTER FLOODING

The large picture shows the junction of the Mississippi and Missouri Rivers in St Louis. The Mississippi runs from top left to bottom right and the Missouri flows from centre left. The small picture shows the same area after heavy rain in 1993. The blue and black areas show floods. Fields, farms and whole sections of the town were flooded, road and railway bridges were swept away, and many thousands of animals were drowned.

Country	People	Environment

Central America

Between North and South America are the Caribbean Islands and a narrow bridge of land. This bridge of land is called Central America. It is made up of eight countries: Mexico, Guatemala, Belize, Costa Rica, El Salvador, Honduras, Nicaragua and Panama. Mexico is four times larger than all the others put together.

In Central America most people are mestizos, a mixture of the native Indians and Europeans. On the Caribbean islands, most people descend from slaves who were brought from Africa in the 18th century to work on plantations. Today, many people work on farms and plantations which grow bananas, sugar cane, cotton and coffee.

Central America is a region of great variety and contrasts. The hot, dry Mexico desert is in the north. Further south is the hot, wet rain forest of Nicaragua and Costa Rica. Thousands of species of plants, insects and animals live here. The islands of the West Indies in the Caribbean Sea stretch in an arc from Florida to Venezuela.

The West Indies
East of Central America are the hundreds of islands in the Caribbean Sea, called the West Indies. Cuba is the largest island. Half the people in the Caribbean live on either Cuba or Haiti. Hurricanes sometimes tear through the Caribbean and Central America. These circular storms start over the sea and head towards land. They can cause great damage. Special weather satellites are used to plot the path of hurricanes.

The growth of tourism
The warm tropical climate of the Caribbean islands and the sandy beaches, palm trees, coral reefs and steep mountains make the Caribbean islands and parts of Mexico a tourist centre. Visitors come from the USA and Canada, as well as from Europe and Japan. Hotels, restaurants, roads and airports have been built for the visitors. Many local people work in the tourist industry.

▲ **This photograph shows air pollution in Mexico City. The city is surrounded by mountains. Fumes from cars and factories become trapped and form a dense smog over the area. Smog is a major problem here.**

The Panama Canal
The narrowest point of Central America is in Panama. An 82 km long canal has been built here to allow ships to sail between the Atlantic and Pacific Oceans. It is an important political and trading route.

Mountains and volcanoes
Central America has volcanoes and mountains, some over 3 000m high. Small earthquakes are common. A flat plateau called the Altiplano lies 2 000m above sea level, between the mountain ranges of Mexico.

Mexico City is built here on the site of Tenochtitlan, the ancient **Aztec** capital. Every week 10 000 people arrive here from the countryside in search of work.

Central America includes 26 different countries. Some, such as St Lucia, consist of just one small island. Others, such as Mexico, are much bigger and stretch over 3 000 km from north to south. The smaller countries sometimes form trading groups to sell their products and to give them greater power.

DID YOU KNOW?

● Mexico covers 1 972 500 sq km. It is about a quarter the size of the USA and eight times bigger than Britain.

● The main languages of the area are Spanish, English and local dialects called patois, which are mixtures of African and English or French.

Central America is a zone which separates the rain forests (seen here in reddish brown) and mountains of South America and the deserts, mountains and plains of North America.

THE BAHAMAS

The Bahamas are a group of low islands off the coast of Florida, USA. This image shows Andros Island with Letuma Sound further away and the Atlantic Ocean beyond. The light blue areas show shallow water and the dark blue areas are channels of deep water.

South America

The Amazon basin is a hot, wet region which has the largest tropical rain forest in the world. This forest contains half of all living species. The thousands of species of plants, insects and animals there may provide cures for diseases such as cancer. But people continue to cut down the forest. The rain forest also prevents soil being washed away, absorbs **carbon dioxide** from the **atmosphere** and helps to control world weather patterns.

The Pampas and beyond
The fertile, flat plains in the south-east part of South America are called the Pampas. Farmers rear cattle here on huge ranches and grow crops of wheat, maize and barley. Further south is the cold desert landscape of Patagonia (Argentina) which is a dry, barren area.

A country of contrasts
Chile is a long, narrow country. Its landscape changes from desert in the north, to a mild Mediterranean-type area in the centre, to a cold, mountainous region in the south. Deep valleys, flooded by the sea, form fiords in the forested south.

The first people to live in South America were tribal Indians such as the Maya of Peru or the Yanomamo of the Amazon rain forest. About 400 years ago explorers and colonists arrived from Spain and Portugal. Most people in South America now speak Portuguese or Spanish, but Indian languages survive in a few places.

The Amazon rain forest in South America is being cleared to create space for cattle ranches and for small farms. In other areas, the forest is cut down for timber or to create space for mines. When the trees are cut down, rain washes away the soil, so the land becomes unusable.

The mountain states
The Andes Mountains run down the western side of South America and are studded with hundreds of volcanoes. The Andes are the source of many streams which drain into the major rivers, such as the Amazon and the Parana. The Andes Mountains occupy parts of Colombia, Ecuador, Venezuela, Peru and Bolivia. The steep hillsides are **terraced** to grow crops such as wheat, coffee and potatoes. Oil has been discovered in the Gulf of Maracaibo, in Venezuela.

◀ **La Paz is one of many cities which developed high in the Andes Mountains where the weather is cooler. It is a fast growing city where most people do not have water piped to their homes.**

▼ **In the desert of northern Chile, valuable minerals such as copper are mined at places like Chuquicamata. Huge holes like the one below are gouged out of the earth during mining.**

COLOMBIA

VENEZUELA

ECUADOR

BRAZIL

PERU

BOLIVIA

N

CHILE

ARGENTINA

PACIFIC OCEAN

ATLANTIC OCEAN

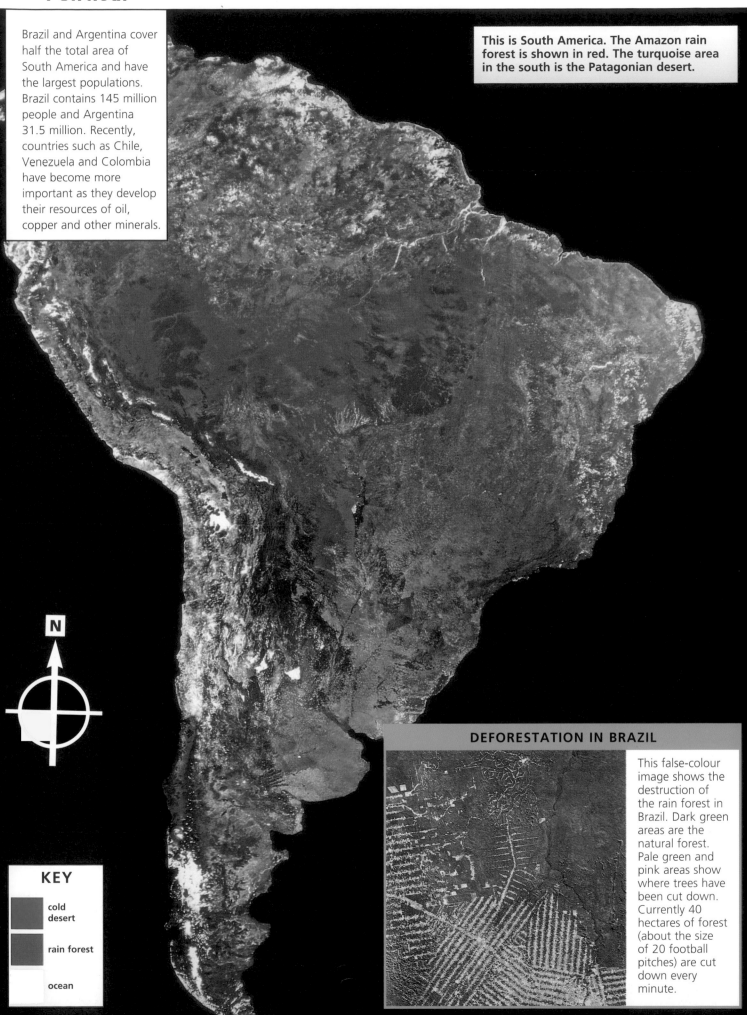

Brazil and Argentina cover half the total area of South America and have the largest populations. Brazil contains 145 million people and Argentina 31.5 million. Recently, countries such as Chile, Venezuela and Colombia have become more important as they develop their resources of oil, copper and other minerals.

This is South America. The Amazon rain forest is shown in red. The turquoise area in the south is the Patagonian desert.

N

KEY

cold desert

rain forest

ocean

DEFORESTATION IN BRAZIL

This false-colour image shows the destruction of the rain forest in Brazil. Dark green areas are the natural forest. Pale green and pink areas show where trees have been cut down. Currently 40 hectares of forest (about the size of 20 football pitches) are cut down every minute.

Canada

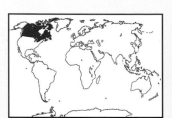

Canada is a huge country. In the west the high Rocky Mountains run parallel to the coast. The peaks are rugged and many are covered by permanent snow and ice. The flat plains of the Prairies run across the centre of the country. To the east the land rises to the vast area of the Canadian Shield, which contains forests, swamps, lakes and minerals such as iron, copper and nickel.

The Great Lakes
The Canada-US border runs through the Great Lakes. These huge areas of water are wide and deep enough for thousands of ships and barges to use.

Rivers and waterfalls
Canada has hundreds of rivers. Some, such as the Nelson, flow north to Hudson Bay or the Arctic Ocean. Others, such as the Fraser River, flow from the Rocky Mountains westwards to the Pacific. The world-famous Niagara Falls are on the Niagara River in the east.

The fish connection
In British Columbia, on the west coast, salmon is caught. On the east coast, Newfoundland is the centre for the fishing industry and cod is the major catch.

The first Canadians were the native Americans and the Inuit (Eskimo). Later, settlers arrived from France and England and spread across the country. Now 45% of Canadians have British ancestry and 29% are of French descent. The remaining 26% are Inuit, native Americans, or people from European countries such as Germany.

In northern Canada, the weather is bitterly cold. In some areas, the ground is permanently frozen. The Arctic Ocean freezes for six months every year. Living conditions here are very harsh. The treeless tundra gives way to vast forests of pine, fir and spruce trees. Further south, the flat Prairies of central Canada are used for wheat growing and cattle grazing.

▲ The Selkirk Mountains in British Columbia, Western Canada, have large areas of forest. The trees are now being cut down and used for timber, wood pulp and paper.

Resource rich
Canada is rich in natural resources. Forest covers one third of the land in Canada and provides wood for valuable exports of furniture, **veneers** and paper. Minerals such as asbestos, iron, gold, lead, zinc, potash, silver and uranium are all found in Canada. Oil and natural gas from Alberta are piped to refineries in Ontario and across the border into the USA.

City life
Eight out of ten Canadians live in cities. Ottawa is the capital, but Toronto is the largest city and the major centre of industry, which ranges from metal smelting to tourism. Quebec is the only city in North America which still has its original town walls. Prairie cities such as Calgary and Saskatchewan have wide streets built on a grid iron pattern. Canada is home to millions of immigrants from all over the world. Its people enjoy a continually rising standard of living.

ARCTIC OCEAN

GREENLAND

ALASKA

N

PACIFIC OCEAN

CANADA

UNITED STATES OF AMERICA

ATLANTIC OCEAN

The border between Canada and the USA is the world's longest land frontier. It stretches 6 416 km and is the longest undefended border in the world. Close links between the USA and Canada mean that there is no need for defences. The rich, powerful USA is Canada's main trading partner and a very important ally.

KEY

coniferous forest

mountains

water

snow/ice

Canada and part of North America can be seen here. Hudson Bay is just above centre. The Great Lakes are below Hudson Bay on the right.

N

VANCOUVER

The city of Vancouver, shown left of centre in pale red, stands on the Pacific coast at the mouth of the River Fraser. It is the centre for the country's growing trade with Japan, South Korea, Singapore and Taiwan in the Far East. The white areas are the mountains and water is shown in dark blue.

MONTREAL

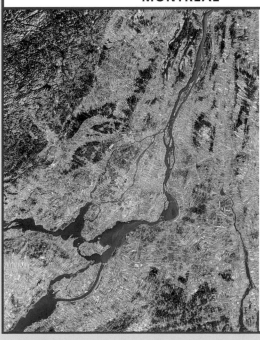

Montreal, the grey area in the centre, is the second largest French-speaking city in the world after Paris. The centre of the city stands on a hill overlooking the St Lawrence river. The river has been dredged and widened to become part of the St Lawrence Seaway which links the Great Lakes with the Atlantic Ocean.

Scandinavia

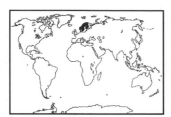

The people of Scandinavia are descendants of the Vikings who lived about 1 000 years ago. The Vikings were seafarers and warriors who travelled to Britain and America. They were also farmers and fishermen. These occupations are still important today. In northern Scandinavia, the **Lapps** herd reindeer across the frontiers of Norway, Sweden and Finland.

The environment varies from country to country. Norway is mountainous and its coastline is dotted with long narrow inlets called fiords. Denmark is low lying and much of the land is farmed. Finland is a land of lakes and forests. Sweden has many forests, mountains and lakes. Iceland is a volcanic island, with hot springs and geysers as well as permanent snow and ice.

Scandinavia is made up of Norway, Sweden, Finland, Denmark and Iceland. The warm waters of the **Gulf Stream** keep Norway's ports ice-free, but there is heavy rain and snow on the coast in winter. Sweden and Finland are drier, but colder in winter and warmer in summer. The Baltic Sea freezes every winter, but ice-breakers keep sea routes open. Further south, Denmark is milder. Iceland, in the North Atlantic, has gales and heavy rainfall.

Natural riches
Scandinavia has many natural resources. The timber industry uses **hydro-electric power** provided by fast-flowing rivers. Iron ore is mined in Sweden. North Sea oil and natural gas are the main exports for Norway.

Danish farms
Denmark has large areas of farmland, producing cattle and pigs. Denmark exports cheese and meat products worldwide.

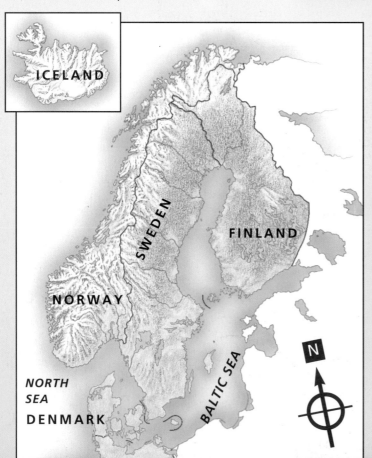

▲ **Wind farms like this one in Denmark have been developed to reduce the need for fuels such as oil, coal and gas. They are pollution-free.**

◄ **Fishing is an important industry in countries such as Norway and Iceland where farmland is in short supply. But so many fish are caught in the Atlantic Ocean and Norwegian Sea that some species, such as herring or cod, may die out.**

Scandinavian industries
Industries such as car making, chemicals, tourism, finance, mining and lumbering, have been developed here. They have produced successful industrial economies and people enjoy a high standard of living.

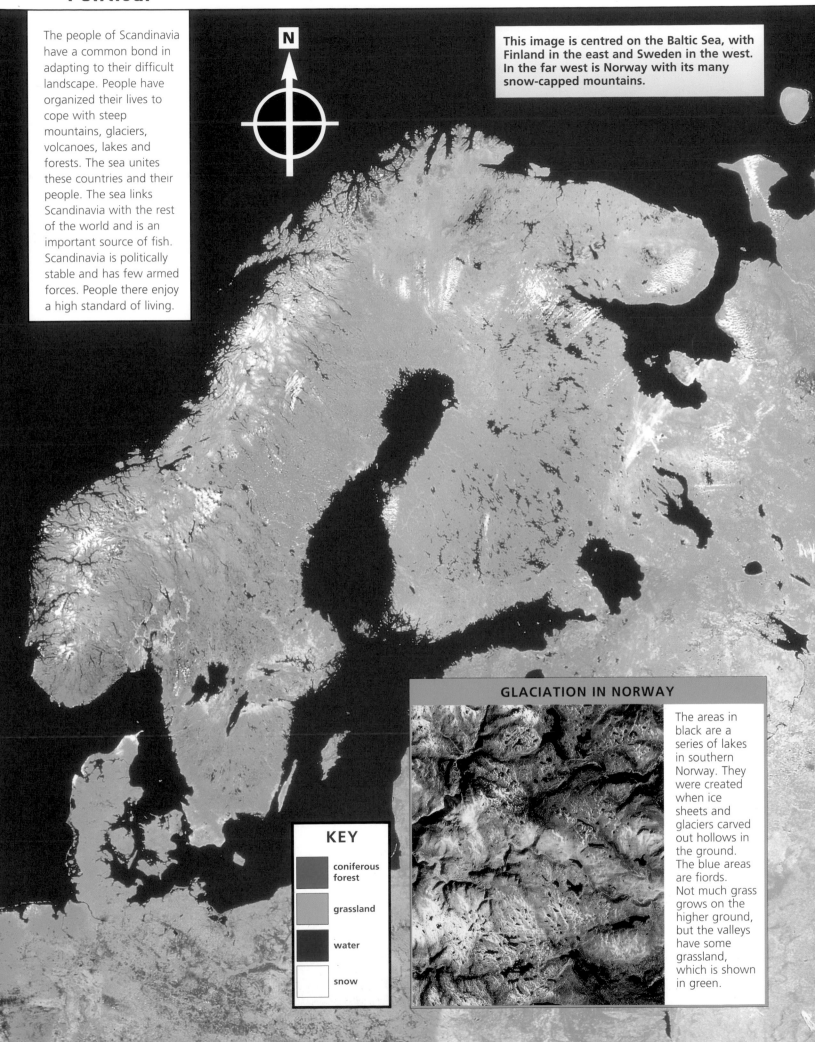

The people of Scandinavia have a common bond in adapting to their difficult landscape. People have organized their lives to cope with steep mountains, glaciers, volcanoes, lakes and forests. The sea unites these countries and their people. The sea links Scandinavia with the rest of the world and is an important source of fish. Scandinavia is politically stable and has few armed forces. People there enjoy a high standard of living.

N

This image is centred on the Baltic Sea, with Finland in the east and Sweden in the west. In the far west is Norway with its many snow-capped mountains.

KEY

- coniferous forest
- grassland
- water
- snow

GLACIATION IN NORWAY

The areas in black are a series of lakes in southern Norway. They were created when ice sheets and glaciers carved out hollows in the ground. The blue areas are fiords. Not much grass grows on the higher ground, but the valleys have some grassland, which is shown in green.

Western Europe

During the 18th and 19th centuries, Western Europe became the first area in the world to experience the **Industrial Revolution**. This brought new wealth to the area. New large-scale industries developed such as steel-making and engineering.

Declining industries
Since the 19th century, some of the older industries such as textiles and shipbuilding have declined. They were unable to compete with cheaper products from countries such as Japan and South Korea.

New industry
New industries such as chemicals, cars and electronics have grown up across Europe. Parts of Europe such as northern France relied on the old industries and now suffer from high unemployment, derelict factories and a polluted environment. Major redevelopment projects are taking place in some of these regions and the rivers, lakes and factories have been cleaned up. New roads and industrial estates are also being built to attract new industries to the area.

During the industrial revolution, many people living in rural areas moved to cities to find work. Now most people in Western Europe live in cities and towns. This depopulation of rural areas has been a cause for concern in some areas such as the Iles de France, where the population is getting older and most of the young people have moved away to find work.

Europe has a varied environment. In the north, the land is flat and forms part of the North European Plain. South of the Alps, the land is hilly with narrow coastal plains. Agriculture and farming are important to the region. Farmers need to be involved in looking after the environment. If they are not, the soil may be eroded and the land scarred for the future.

The European Union
Fifteen European countries: Austria, Belgium, France, Finland, Denmark, Germany, Greece, Ireland, Italy, Spain, Sweden, Luxembourg, Portugal, the Netherlands and the UK have joined together to form the European Union (EU). The aim of the EU is to unite the resources of all its members into a single powerful economy and to encourage free trade between the EU member countries.

New members
The success of the EU in developing economic growth has encouraged other nations, such as Turkey, Malta, Cyprus and Switzerland, to want to join the union. The headquarters of the EU is in Brussels and the European Parliament, which is made up of representatives from the member countries, meets in Strasbourg.

▲ This European stock market links traders all over the world. Computers are used to buy and sell shares quickly.

▼ The Channel Tunnel now links Britain with the rest of Europe. The London–Paris journey takes only three hours.

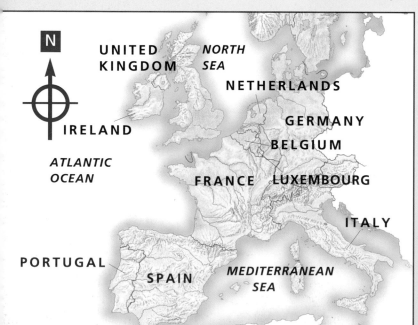

N

UNITED KINGDOM   NORTH SEA
NETHERLANDS
IRELAND   GERMANY
                         BELGIUM
ATLANTIC OCEAN
         FRANCE   LUXEMBOURG

                              ITALY

PORTUGAL
         SPAIN   MEDITERRANEAN SEA

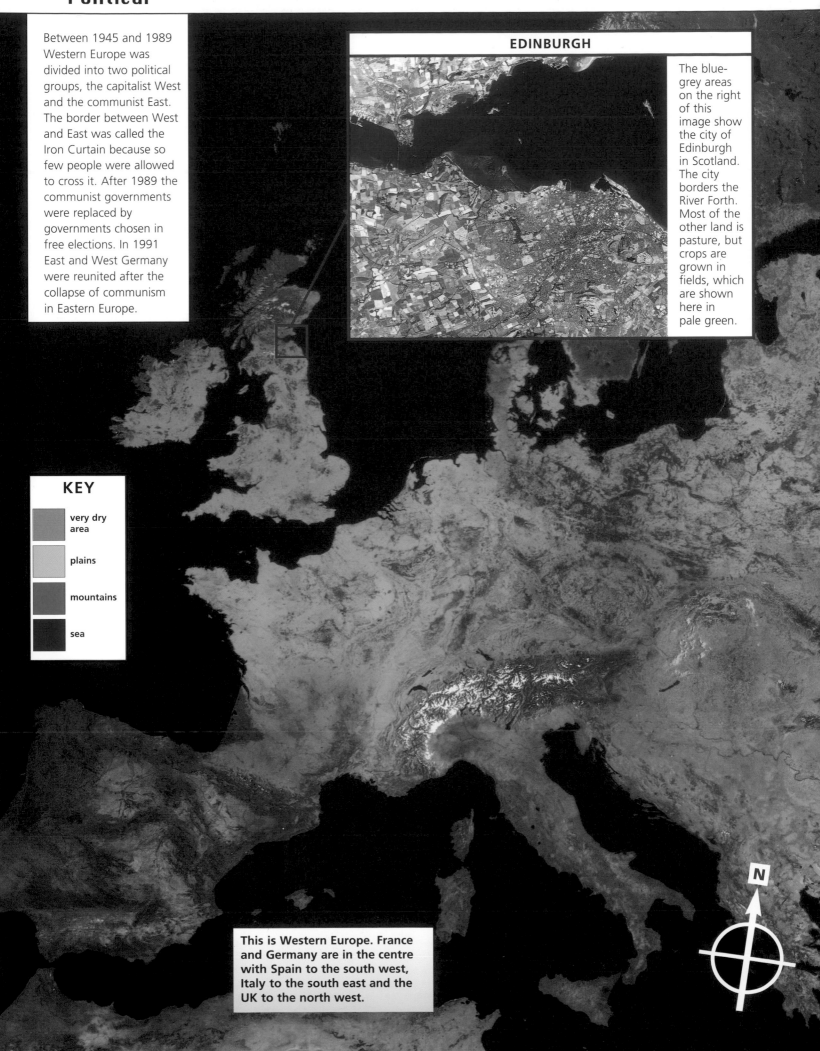

Between 1945 and 1989 Western Europe was divided into two political groups, the capitalist West and the communist East. The border between West and East was called the Iron Curtain because so few people were allowed to cross it. After 1989 the communist governments were replaced by governments chosen in free elections. In 1991 East and West Germany were reunited after the collapse of communism in Eastern Europe.

EDINBURGH

The blue-grey areas on the right of this image show the city of Edinburgh in Scotland. The city borders the River Forth. Most of the other land is pasture, but crops are grown in fields, which are shown here in pale green.

KEY

- very dry area
- plains
- mountains
- sea

This is Western Europe. France and Germany are in the centre with Spain to the south west, Italy to the south east and the UK to the north west.

N

Western Europe

Western Europe is on the western side of the Euro-Asian landmass. Areas in the west, such as the UK have mild, wet winters and cool summers. Countries further inland, such as Germany and Austria have cold winters and hot summers. The countries around the Mediterranean Sea enjoy mild, wet winters and hot dry summers.

Farming patterns

The varied climate and different types of landscape in Western Europe, ranging from mountains to plains, have led to a wide variety of farming patterns in the region.

Valuable crops

Countries such as Italy, and Spain enjoy a warm Mediterranean climate which is suitable for growing grapes, olives, fruit and fresh vegetables. These crops are valuable and need to reach markets quickly. They are often sent by air to the cities of northern Europe such as London and Berlin.

From pigs to barley

The cooler, wetter countries of northern Europe such as the Netherlands, the UK and Germany concentrate on rearing cattle, sheep and pigs and growing grain such as wheat, barley or oil-seed rape.

Raw materials

Farming is important in this part of the world because it provides the raw material for industries such as sugar refining, which employs thousands of people.

Drainage and irrigation

In many parts of Europe extra farmland has been created by draining wetland or by irrigating dry regions. In the Netherlands land has been reclaimed from the sea. The land is criss-crossed with drainage ditches which carry away the water. The reclaimed land is used to grow sugar beet, potatoes, wheat and grass for dairy cattle. Flower bulbs are grown in areas with sandy soil.

In the drier parts of southern Europe, such as Italy, dams have been built on rivers to form lakes. The water is then used to irrigate the land and grow fruits such as strawberries, oranges and grapefruit and crops such as tobacco, rice and cotton.

▲ Vine growing is important in many areas of Western Europe such as Bordeaux in France (see above). In recent years, the European Union (EU) has given grants to farmers to destroy poor vines and plant new better quality varieties. Most grapes are still harvested by hand.

◄ Benidorm in Spain is a favourite resort for holiday-makers seeking sun and sea. The beach is backed by tall apartment blocks and hotels.

The tourist industry

Tourism is very important in Western Europe. There are three main types of tourist destinations. Some people go to areas such as the Costa Brava in Spain where they can be sure of finding sun, sand and sea. Others visit historic towns and cities such as Edinburgh, Ghent, Paris and Amsterdam.

Areas of outstanding natural beauty, such as the west of Ireland, the Black Forest in Germany and mountain areas such as the Alps attract tourists. In mountain areas, skiing is the main attraction during winter, while in summer, hiking and climbing are the main activities. Other popular tourist destinations are spa towns, such as Spa in Belgium where visitors go to visit the historic sites as well as to experience the refreshing baths.

BORDEAUX

Bordeaux in south-west France is an important area for the wine industry and tourism. The city is shown in pale pink and is right of centre. The River Garonne runs through the city and joins the River Dordogne to form the Gironde estuary. There are vineyards both east and west of the Gironde. The beach is shown as a pale line on the far left.

This multi-coloured image is of the Bay of Naples, one of the most beautiful parts of southern Italy. Mount Vesuvius, an ancient volcano, can be seen right of centre. The city of Naples is left of the volcano. The roads, rivers and mountains of the area can be clearly seen.

Eastern Europe

Eastern Europe is a mixture of mountains, valleys and plains such as the flat North European Plain in Poland. The Ore and Tatra mountains separate central and northern parts of Eastern Europe.

Offshore islands
The Hungarian Plain is a broad lowland with the Balkan mountains to the south and the Transylvanian Alps in the east. In former Yugoslavia, mountains run parallel to the coast. Rises in sea level here have flooded valleys and created offshore islands on the Dalmatian coast.

Weather and climate
Greece and Croatia have moderate climates. Elsewhere, winters are cold and snowy. Summers are hot and sunny with occasional storms. Greece, Bosnia, Croatia and Slovenia have mild wet winters and hot dry summers.

Varied crops
In the north, crops such as potatoes, wheat and barley are grown and sheep, cattle and pigs are reared. In the south, vines are grown in Greece, Bulgaria and Croatia to produce wine for export.

Eastern Europe has a mixture of many ethnic groups, such as Greeks, Serbs and Croats. Greek civilization is very old and Greek philosophers have influenced people all over the world. Religion varies from place to place. Poland is Roman Catholic, while the Orthodox Church is important in Greece and Serbia. The Muslim faith has many followers in Bosnia, Albania and Turkey.

The land, air and water in Eastern Europe are badly polluted. Acid rain has destroyed trees all over the region and huge holes in the ground have been made by open-cast mining. Toxic waste often fills these abandoned holes or has been dumped into streams, rivers and lakes. Air pollution in some parts of Poland is so bad that, on some days, people are warned not to go out.

Farming problems
Most farms do not use modern farming techniques such as chemical sprays to control insect pests. Many cannot afford expensive modern equipment such as combine harvesters and deep ploughs. In the past, communist state planners channelled money into developing heavy industries such as iron, steel and engineering. This meant that farming was deprived of the vital money and resources it needed to develop. Today, many farming jobs are still done by hand and many crops are still transported in carts pulled by horses.

▲ **The Blue Mosque in Turkey is one of the main centres of the Islamic religion in Eastern Europe. Priests call the people to prayer from the tall thin towers called minarets.**

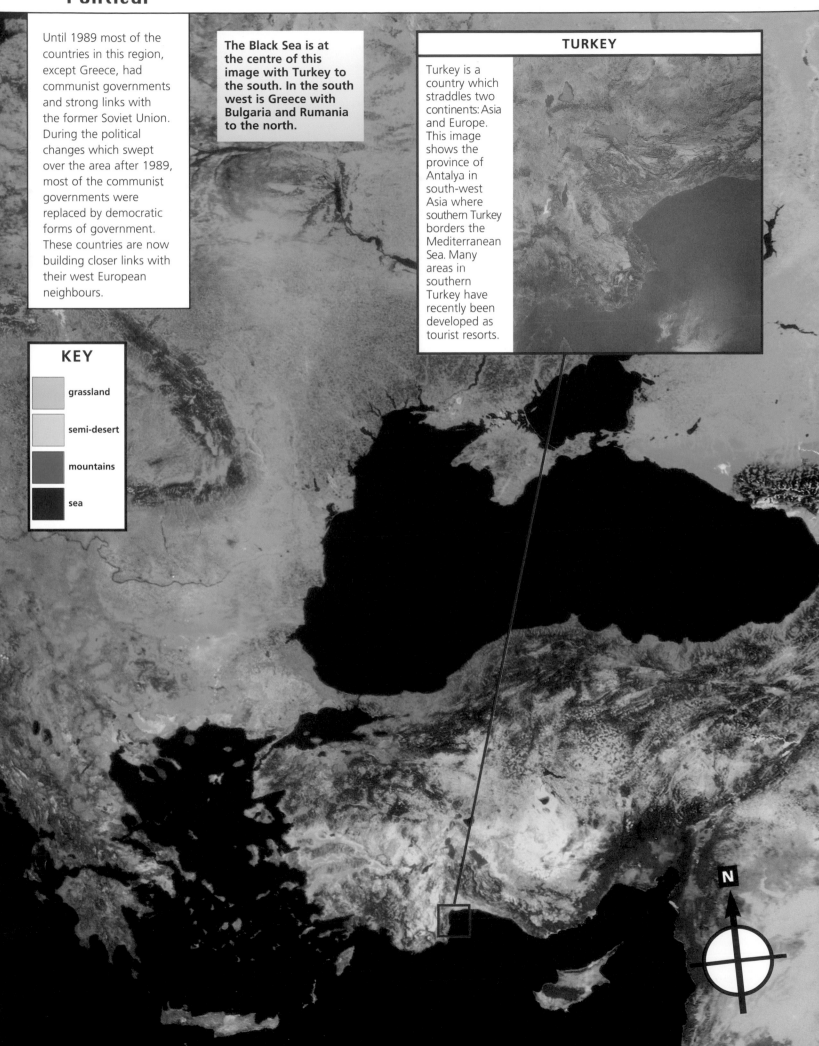

Until 1989 most of the countries in this region, except Greece, had communist governments and strong links with the former Soviet Union. During the political changes which swept over the area after 1989, most of the communist governments were replaced by democratic forms of government. These countries are now building closer links with their west European neighbours.

The Black Sea is at the centre of this image with Turkey to the south. In the south west is Greece with Bulgaria and Rumania to the north.

TURKEY

Turkey is a country which straddles two continents: Asia and Europe. This image shows the province of Antalya in south-west Asia where southern Turkey borders the Mediterranean Sea. Many areas in southern Turkey have recently been developed as tourist resorts.

KEY

grassland

semi-desert

mountains

sea

Eastern Europe

During the 1960s and 70s in Poland, Czechoslovakia, Greece and Bulgaria, industries such as iron, steel, chemicals and engineering expanded.

From locomotives to explosives
Czechoslovakia was the most industrialized country in Eastern Europe and had a tradition of engineering which produces everything from railway locomotives to Semtex explosive. The country is now divided into two separate states: the Czech Republic, where most of the industry is found, and Slovakia.

More power
The growth in industry needed increasing amounts of electric power. In Poland and the Czech Republic, deposits of brown coal (lignite) are burned in power stations. This creates serious air pollution and increases the number of asthma sufferers and lung cancer victims in the region.

Hydro-electricity
Countries such as the Czech Republic, Slovakia and Hungary built dams along rivers such as the Danube to generate hydro-electric power. These nations cannot

▲ This area has been polluted by the Eleshuitsa copper mine in Bulgaria. The landscape will never recover.

agree a plan to build more dams so developments have stopped. Romania, Bulgaria and Hungary have built nuclear power stations to provide electricity.

Radioactive leaks
Eastern European nuclear power stations have had problems with safety standards which scientists are now working to improve. The risk is that radioactivity may leak from the power stations or from **contaminated** waste and pollute the surrounding area.

Widespread modernization
Investment from other countries is helping to modernize old factories and clean up the pollution. Western European companies are building new factories to assemble cars because wage rates in the area are low. There is a growing demand for cars and consumer goods such as washing machines.

New tourism
Eastern Europe has begun to develop its coastline in order to expand its tourist industry. Southern Turkey is now a popular area for holidaymakers from the West. Other areas of tourist development are ancient towns and cities such as Istanbul in northern Turkey.

▲ The Black Sea is now a popular holiday resort for thousands of people from both Western and Eastern Europe. The sun, sand and sea resorts are competition for traditional Mediterranean holiday areas such as Spain and Greece.

► Agriculture in many parts of Eastern Europe has not yet been modernized and many farmers use horse-drawn vehicles. Farmers need tractors, trucks and combine harvesters to produce enough food for the countries' rapidly growing populations.

KEY

lowland plains

mountains

sea

DID YOU KNOW?

● Budapest with 3.9 million people and Athens with 3.1 million are the two largest cities in Eastern Europe.

● The Danube is the longest river, running 2 858 km from Germany to the Black Sea.

● Musala in Bulgaria is the highest mountain at 2 925m.

N

The Baltic Sea is in the north of this image with the Adriatic Sea to the south west. The Carpathian mountains lie in the centre of the image between the two seas.

Country

Northern Africa

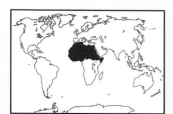

Africa is a huge plateau, broken by just a few mountain ranges such as the Atlas Mountains of Algeria. In some places, especially on the north and west coasts, a narrow coastal plain stretches along the edge of the plateau. Africa is the world's warmest continent.

Different environments
The southern part of this region is an area of tropical rain forest and has a hot, wet, **equatorial** climate. Areas of forest have been cleared either for timber or to create farmland for the rapidly growing population.

In the countries north of the Sahara Desert, most people speak Arabic. To the south and east there is a wide range of ethnic groups with their own languages, customs and religions. Nomadic groups such as the Tuareg still wander the Sahara with their animals in search of water and pasture. Some now have motor bikes and radios, but their way of life remains similar to their ancestors.

The Sahara Desert covers 9 million sq km and is the world's largest desert. The desert surface varies from sand-dunes to pebbles, to bare rock. The climate is so dry that only a few plants (such as the cactus) and animals (such as the desert rat) can survive. Along the northern and southern edges of the Sahara the climate is wetter and crops such as cotton, grapes and dates are grown.

The savannas of Africa
North of the Equator, the climate is drier and the forest is replaced by tropical grassland. These are the savannas of Africa, which are found in western countries such as Niger and Ivory Coast. Herds of zebra and gazelle lived on these savannas, as well as predators such as lion and hyena which feed on other animals. The herds were all killed and now crops such as cotton, groundnuts and coffee are grown here.

Flowers in the desert
The Sahara is a vast, hot desert. Occasionally, rain falls in short, torrential downpours and the desert bursts into bloom. Seeds which have waited for years suddenly flower and complete their life cycle in a few weeks.

Coastal areas
The coastal areas of North and West Africa have more rainfall. Grapes, wheat, maize, barley and citrus fruits are grown here. The long, sandy beaches and hot, sunny summers have made countries such as the Gambia and Egypt important centres of tourism.

▲ **Irrigated farming has become more and more important as the population of countries such as Niger has grown. Rainfall is often unreliable so crops from irrigated farms are vital to the country's economy.**

▲ **Nine-tenths of Egypt is desert so its people depend on water from the River Nile to irrigate their crops. This village is built at the entrance to the Valley of the Dead above irrigated sugar cane fields.**

Northern Africa has some of the poorest countries in the world, such as Burkina Faso, Mali, Ethiopia and Sudan. In recent years there have been severe famines in some of these countries and food aid has been sent from Europe, the USA and the rest of the world. The most powerful countries in the region are Nigeria, Ghana and Morocco, because they are rich in resources.

▼ **Northern Africa is dominated by the Sahara Desert. South of the Sahara are the green savanna grasslands and further south still are the rain forests of Nigeria and Zaire.**

ALGERIA

The nuclear reactor at Ain Oussera, in Algeria is shown as the black area on the left of this image. Algeria is using nuclear power to generate electricity to use as fuel for its development programme.

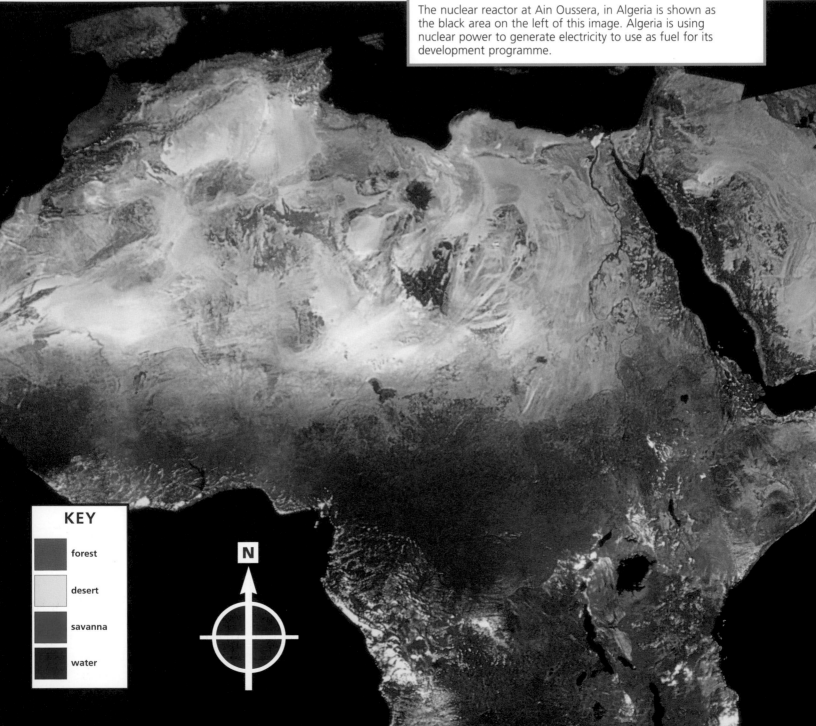

KEY

- forest
- desert
- savanna
- water

N

Northern Africa

The Sahara Desert now extends north and south into land that used to be cultivated. This is the result of **desertification**, which is caused by a combination of unreliable rainfall and human interference. In some places in West Africa, such as Mali and Burkina Faso, too many animals are reared on poor pasture.

In these countries, wealth is judged by the number of animals a person owns, so it is hard to persuade people to keep fewer animals. These herds trample the fragile grassland on the edges of the Sahara and the grass dies, unable to recover. The thin soil becomes exposed, blows away and becomes sand. The Sahel, along the southern edge of the Sahara, is an area of desertification.

The Nile

The river Nile is in north-east Africa and is vital to Ethiopia, Sudan and Egypt. The river provides water for irrigation to produce crops for millions of people.

Loss of trees

Many trees have been cut down in Ethiopia. Rainwater now carries away vital top soil every time rain falls. Further downstream, giant dams, such as Egypt's Aswan dam, create lakes to store water for irrigation and to generate hydro-electricity. The lake is now gradually becoming shallower as it silts up with the soil carried down from Ethiopia.

Mineral wealth

Northern Africa is rich in minerals. Some are found in the desert and some in the rain forest. Iron ore from Mauritania is exported all over the world. Libya, Algeria and Nigeria all have large reserves of oil and natural gas. This has made these countries richer than other countries in the region, although oil prices rise and fall from year to year.

The risk of pollution

Oil-rich countries have used the money from oil exports to build new industries including chemicals and textiles, and to develop modern cities such as Accra and Tripoli. But the discovery of oil means there is a constant risk of pollution from oil spills in drilling areas such as the delta of the River Niger. Oil slicks from supertankers loading on the coasts of west or north Africa are also a danger.

The Red Sea

The Red Sea marks the point at which Arabia split away from Africa millions of years ago. The construction of the Suez Canal in the 1860s linked the Mediterranean Sea to the Red Sea and since then ships have been able to sail from Europe to Asia without going around the whole of Africa.

▲ The discovery of oil in the Niger Delta has brought wealth to this country. Some waterways have been seriously polluted and local tribes have been forced to move by drilling operations.

▶ This is an area in Mali, West Africa which is threatened by the spread of desert sand. Desertification is a constant problem in the region. In some areas, trees have been planted as an experiment to try to prevent the topsoil from blowing away.

NILE DELTA

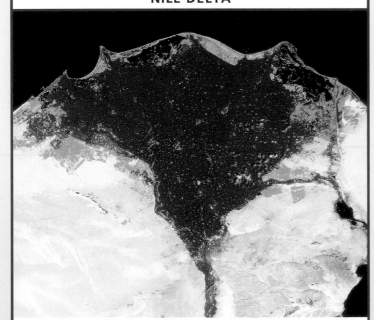

False colours have been used in this stunning image of the Nile delta where it enters the Mediterranean Sea. The large red area is agricultural land. The green areas near the coast are lagoons and wetlands which have been partly reclaimed. The bright pink area shows the town of Alexandria spreading into the desert. The light grey area just below centre is Egypt's capital city, Cairo.

LAKE NASSER AND ASWAN DAM

This satellite photograph shows the point where the River Nile, shown here in the top half of the image, flows out of Lake Nasser in southern Egypt, shown here in the lower half of the image. The Aswan Dam can be seen just above centre of the photograph. Lake Nasser is the world's second largest artificial lake and is 500 km long.

Central and Southern Africa

There are many different black African peoples in this region, such as the Baka tribe of the rain forest, who are the smallest people in the world. The Bushmen of the Kalahari Desert live a traditional life hunting animals and collecting berries and roots. The 5 million white people in the region came originally from the UK and the Netherlands and now live in South Africa, Zambia and Zimbabwe.

The Great Rift Valley of East Africa cuts deep into the African plateau and is dotted with lakes and volcanoes. It was formed centuries ago when land slipped down between two great faults in the Earth's crust. Scientists think the area east of the Rift Valley may eventually break away, just as the island of Madagascar, off the east coast, broke away from the continent 50 million years ago.

Central and Southern Africa have a wide range of environments, from the tropical rain forests of Zaire to the desert of the Kalahari and the vast savanna grasslands of East Africa. Herds of zebra, giraffe and wildebeest roam these grasslands. In the middle of the savannas are the high snow-capped peaks of Mount Kenya and Mount Kilimanjaro. The discovery of diamonds in the Kalahari Desert, which covers most of Botswana and Namibia, has led to the building of roads, airstrips and towns.

Mineral wealth

Copper was discovered in Zaire and Zambia in the 19th century and has been mined ever since. The Kariba Dam was built on the Zambezi River to provide hydro-electric power for the mines, railways and towns of Zambia and Zimbabwe. Behind the dam Lake Kariba has flooded a huge area of farmland that stretches back almost as far as the Victoria Falls.

Tropical rain forest

The African rain forest has many species of trees, plants, insects and animals. Parts of the forest have been cut down to create space for new farmland or mining. The gorillas that live there are dying out because of hunting and the cutting down of trees. The clearing of the forest started when the local population grew and needed more and more farmland. Korup National Park has been established to pr

▼ **The Victoria Falls on the River Zambezi are one of the most spectacular sights in Africa. The river tumbles 120 metres into a deep gorge. The falls are now a major tourist attraction.**

Most countries in this area were colonies of European countries during the 19th and early 20th centuries. They have only recently been able to break free from their colonial links and become independent countries. South Africa is the most recent country to grant freedom to all its people irrespective of their skin colour.

N

MOUNT KILIMANJARO

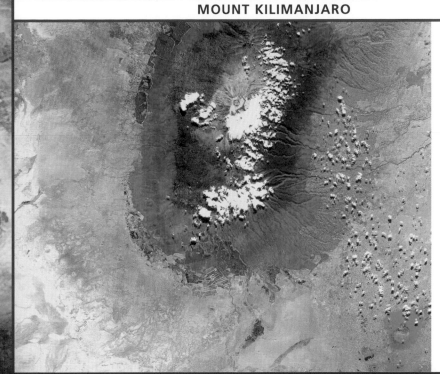

This is a bird's eye view of the crater on top of Mount Kilimanjaro which is a volcano on the border of Kenya and Tanzania. It is Africa's highest mountain and rises to 5 896m. The dark green shows the forests clinging to the slopes of the mountain and streams can be seen draining away from the summit. The white areas are cloud.

KEY

- forest
- desert
- savanna
- water

DID YOU KNOW?

● Madagascar has been cut off from the rest of Africa for so long that it now has plants and animals not found anywhere else in the world.

● The Zaire is the longest river in the region and is 4 667 km long.

● The smallest country in Africa is Comoros, a tiny island between Madagascar and Mozambique.

● Lake Victoria is the biggest lake in Africa and covers 69 400 sq km.

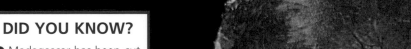

This is a satellite image of Central and Southern Africa, with Madagascar off the east coast.

Central & Southern Africa

South Africa and Namibia are world-famous producers of gold and diamonds. Diamonds are found along the long sandy coast of Namibia. They were deposited there centuries ago by rivers from the interior. Now huge grab shovels scoop up sand and pass it through a series of sieves to separate the diamonds from the sand.

Diamond mines

In areas such as Kimberley in South Africa, diamonds are mined deep underground, where they are hidden in a layer of blue clay. The search for new deposits continues. The De Beers company of South Africa is one of the world's major suppliers of diamonds, which are used as cutting tools in industry and in jewellery.

▲ Gold mining is very important in South Africa. Miners work in hot, cramped conditions deep underground in order to extract the gold bearing rocks. It is hard, dangerous work.

Gold mines

The gold mines of South Africa are famous the world over. Huge spoil heaps of earth are dumped around the mines which go deeper and deeper in search of gold.

From peaches to ostrich feathers

There are areas of fertile farmland in Zambia, Zimbabwe and South Africa. Some of this land is irrigated and crops of grapes, apples, pears, peaches, wheat, maize, cotton and tobacco are grown.

Sheep are reared in drier areas and ostrich farms provide feathers for the fashion industry and meat. Every few years serious droughts cause crops to die and waterholes to dry up. This has a serious effect on wildlife such as rhino and elephants as well as on farms where crops fail.

South Africa and apartheid

A minority of white people used to rule South Africa under a system called apartheid. In those days the black majority had no right to vote and were forced to live in the poorest parts of the country. Now all people in South Africa have a right to vote. Apartheid has ended and a democratically-elected government rules the country. The biggest farms are still owned by white people but this is now beginning to change as black people get their fair share of the country's resources.

National game parks

Tourism is a growth industry in Central and Southern Africa. The main attractions are the game parks. These are often National Parks such as the Ngorogoro Crater and the Okavango delta in which the wildlife is protected. Visitors travel in tourist minibuses or independently in four wheel drive jeeps to see the area's wild animals, such as lion, giraffe, cheetah and impala. The income from tourism is used to build new roads and houses for local people. Kenya, Tanzania and Uganda are in the savanna grasslands zone and have a thriving tourist industry based on wildlife safaris.

Cities and shanty towns

There are large modern cities such as Johannesburg, Nairobi and Bulawayo in Central and Southern Africa. High-rise office blocks crowd the city centres and rush-hour traffic jams are a fact of life. Further from the centre, factories mix with residential suburbs. Shanty towns are common on the outskirts of these cities.

◄ This is Nairobi, the capital of Kenya. The centre of Nairobi has tall office blocks and hotels typical of most large modern cities. Factories are built on roads leading out of the city centre.

▲ The grassy plains of East Africa provide ideal conditions for all types of wildlife, from zebra to lion and cheetah. The animals attract thousands of tourists every year. These tourists are on safari in the Ngorogoro Crater.

Just above centre we can see sunlight glinting off the Okavango River in the Kalahari desert in Botswana. The river flows into an inland delta called the Okavango swamp. Water is trapped in the delta but most of it evaporates in the desert heat. Further north, in Angola, the smoke from fires on the savanna grasslands is visible.

KEY

water

desert

smoke

CAPE PENINSULA

This false colour image of the area around Cape Town shows ...ops in red, and urban areas in light blue. Cape Town is at ... top of the Cape Peninsula. At the bottom of the peninsula ...he Cape of Good Hope. The dark area next to Cape Town ...able Mountain which reaches 1 086m. The steep edge of ...African plateau can be seen in the top right hand area.

South-West Asia

South-west Asia lies at the meeting point of three continents – Asia, Africa and Europe. It has a wide range of environments, from the harsh desert sands of Arabia to the wetter Mediterranean coasts of Turkey, Syria, Israel and Lebanon.

Making the desert bloom

In Israel, people have changed the desert environment to grow food and other crops. Water from the River Jordan has been diverted to hundreds of irrigation canals which carry it to the fields. The amount of water sent to each field is controlled and huge sheets of black plastic are used to cover lakes and reservoirs to prevent evaporation. Fruit such as oranges and strawberries and vegetables such as celery and avocadoes are now grown in areas that were once desert. Israel exports fruit and vegetables to western Europe.

Sun, sand and civilizations

The hot, sunny summers of the Mediterranean coast from Turkey to Israel have made this area a favourite tourist spot. Sandy beaches, steep cliffs and the ruins of ancient civilizations are added attractions.

Most people in this region are Arabs. They are Muslims and followers of Islam. They speak the Arabic language and worship in mosques. Iran and Turkey are non-Arabic countries but they are Muslim. They worship the god Allah and his prophet Muhammed who was born 1400 years ago in Mecca, Saudi Arabia. Some people from Cyprus and Lebanon are Christian. Most Israelis follow the Jewish faith.

This is a region of great contrasts. The Fertile Crescent is the area between the Tigris and Euphrates rivers. The world's first farming communities settled here among ancient peoples such as the Assyrians and Babylonians. In sharp contrast is the hot desert of the Arabian peninsula. The mountain areas of the north have a cooler, wetter climate and run from Turkey, east and south into Iran.

▼ **The streets in the old city of Jerusalem are narrow where the stone buildings crowd together. Small spaces are used by stall holders selling fruit, vegetables and food.**

▲ **Gold and jewellery are very important to everyone in Iran. Here a woman in traditional black robes scans the shelves of a modern jewellery store.**

Too many tourists

More than 1 million people visit the area every year. Hotels, restaurants, roads, marinas, airports and golf courses have been built for tourists. Remote areas have been invaded by the visitors and not everyone is happy about it. Some local people make money from souvenirs or by working in hotels. Others complain about the influence of western culture on the are

Lebanon at war

The Lebanon used to attract tourists, but its long and bloody civil w means that now most visitors go to Israel, Turkey, Cyprus or Syri

BLACK SEA

CASPIAN SEA

TURKEY

MEDITERRANEAN SEA

SYRIA

LEBANON

IRAQ

IRAN

ISRAEL

JORDAN

SAUDI ARABIA

UNITED ARAB EMIRATES

OMAN

YEMEN

N

RED SEA

ARABIAN SEA

This region is sometimes called The Middle East. It has a reputation for conflict. The island of Cyprus, for example, is divided in two, following the Turkish invasion in 1974. The main conflicts in the regions have been between Israel and its Arab neighbours; between Iran and Iraq; and between Iraq and Kuwait.

Right of centre is the Sea of Galilee in northern Israel. The River Jordan runs from north to south through the area.

DEAD SEA

This is the Dead Sea with the River Jordan flowing into it from the north. The Dead Sea is very salty, and is shrinking as a result of evaporation. The light blue areas at the bottom of the image are shallow areas which will soon be dry. Jerusalem is the tiny grey-blue area left of the Dead Sea.

KEY

highland

arable land

sea

South-West Asia

Parts of South-west Asia are mountainous, especially in northern Iran, Iraq and eastern Turkey. The Kurdish people live in these mountains and form an ethnic group which spreads across three countries. They have tried to create a separate state with their own culture and way of life, but have been attacked by Iraq and Turkey.

The discovery of oil

The discovery of oil in Saudi Arabia, Kuwait, Iran, Iraq, Oman and the United Arab Emirates has made these countries powerful. Oil strikes in the 1920s were followed by more in the 1950s and 60s. The demand for oil increased as the car became a more common form of transport. More oil wells were sunk and new pipelines carried the oil to newly-built ports such as Abadan.

Spending oil money

The oil-rich countries had to decide how to use their new wealth. Most rebuilt parts of towns and cities. Others built completely new towns in the harsh desert. Oil paid for new towns, roads, airports, power stations and sports stadia.

Providing water

Drinking water was scarce in some areas so some of the oil money was spent on building dams and sinking wells to provide water for irrigated farming. Saudi Arabia built special plants to change sea water into drinking water. These desalinization plants are expensive but they provide a way of using local sea water.

New land

On the coast, land has been reclaimed from shallow marine areas. Oil revenues have also provided valuable new land around key ports such as Dubai and Abu Dhabi. This land is used as docks or for industrial development.

The future of oil

World oil prices rise and fall. The oil countries form a body called OPEC (the Organization of Petroleum Exporting Countries). Members meet regularly to set a world price for oil. Oil countries know that oil will one day run out so they invest in new industries such as electronics to provide income when the oil has gone.

▲ The discovery of oil in this region has transformed small, poverty-stricken states into wealthy countries. Here an oil rig in the United Arab Emirates continues the search for new oil fields.

▼ Minority groups such as the Kurds in northern Iraq are often persecuted. These people are refugees who have been forced to flee from their homes by soldiers.

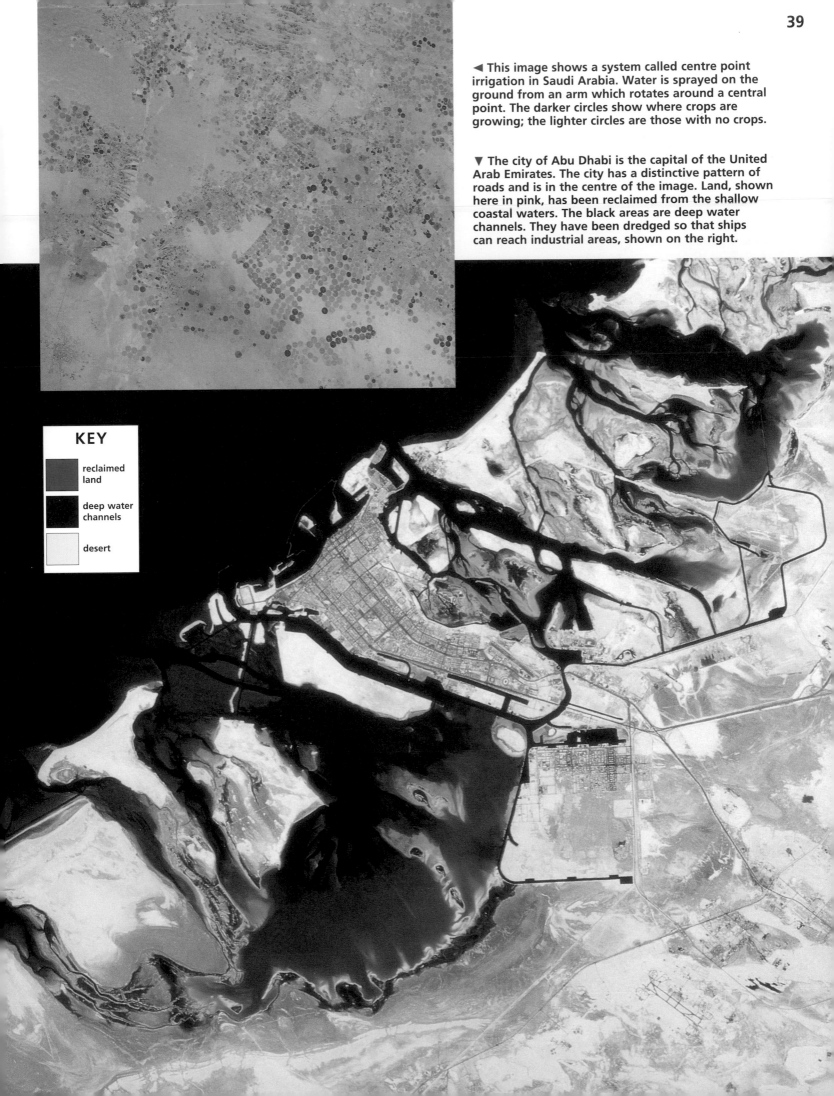

◄ This image shows a system called centre point irrigation in Saudi Arabia. Water is sprayed on the ground from an arm which rotates around a central point. The darker circles show where crops are growing; the lighter circles are those with no crops.

▼ The city of Abu Dhabi is the capital of the United Arab Emirates. The city has a distinctive pattern of roads and is in the centre of the image. Land, shown here in pink, has been reclaimed from the shallow coastal waters. The black areas are deep water channels. They have been dredged so that ships can reach industrial areas, shown on the right.

KEY

■ reclaimed land

■ deep water channels

□ desert

Russia and its neighbours

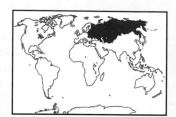

Russia spreads across two continents and is divided by the Ural Mountains, with Europe in the west and Asia in the east. The European part occupies less than 20% of the total land area but more than 70% of the people live there. This is because the climate in the east is very severe. Siberia is part of this vast region and winter temperatures here can fall to -45°C. Even in summer, some areas of the sub-soil stay frozen. Pine, fir and spruce forests spread across Siberia to the Pacific coast. Further north, barren, treeless tundra fringes the Arctic Ocean.

Industrial change

In 1917 Russia had few industries. Most people lived on the land as peasant farmers. The communist government built steel works and engineering factories, opened coal mines and drilled oil wells. Russia is now a major industrial power. But Russian industry needs up to date equipment to modernize its industries and cut down on pollution.

Siberian storehouse

Siberia is an area of vast untapped resources. Huge forests, deposits of coal, oil, natural gas, diamonds, gold, iron ore and other minerals are found here. Only the oil and gas have been exploited so far, but Russia will go on to develop Siberia's other resources.

This area used to be called the Soviet Union (USSR). Today, the 15 communist Republics are independent countries. Russia is the largest and dominates the region. There are more than 100 different national groups in the area, many with their own language and customs. Russian is spoken by the largest number of people. In the south most people are Muslims and follow the Islamic faith.

The pollution here is one of the world's most serious problems. The former communist government focused on industrial production at all costs. Factories were allowed to pollute the air, land and water as long as they met production targets. The massive leak of radioactive waste from the Chernobyl nuclear power station in 1986 showed how damaging this pollution is.

The severe climate and lack of roads and railways here makes development difficult, but as the world runs out of resources, these problems will be overcome.

The growth of tourism

Tourism is growing as more people from abroad visit Russia's old cathedrals and ancient cities.

◀ **This woman is one of the Buryat people. She is wearing traditional dress. Under communist rule, wearing this kind of dress was forbidden. Communist rule ended in 1991. The woman remembered the dress and made it herself.**

LITHUANIA

LATVIA

ESTONIA

BELARUS

ARCTIC OCEAN

■ Moscow

RUSSIA

UKRAINE

MOLDOVA

KAZAKHSTAN

GEORGIA

N

▲ **The onion-shaped domes of St Basil's Cathedral in Moscow are world famous. Every year thousands of tourists come to visit the cathedral. There has been renewed interest in religion since the end of communism.**

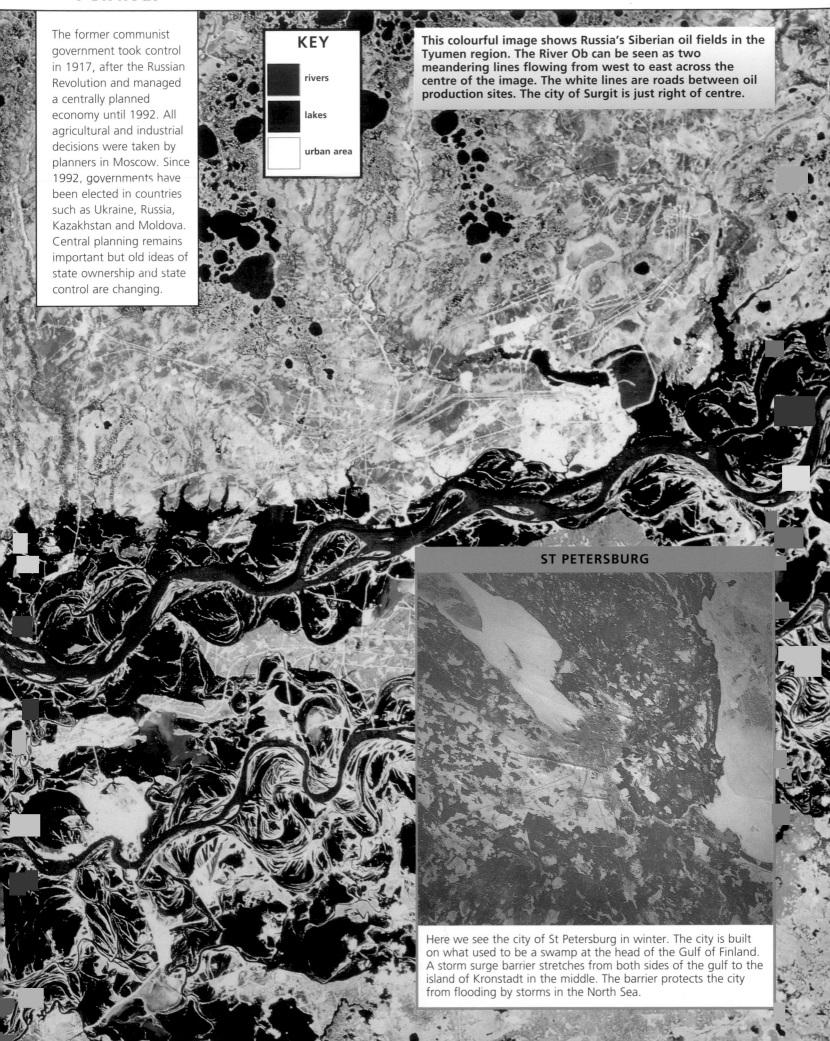

The former communist government took control in 1917, after the Russian Revolution and managed a centrally planned economy until 1992. All agricultural and industrial decisions were taken by planners in Moscow. Since 1992, governments have been elected in countries such as Ukraine, Russia, Kazakhstan and Moldova. Central planning remains important but old ideas of state ownership and state control are changing.

KEY

rivers

lakes

urban area

This colourful image shows Russia's Siberian oil fields in the Tyumen region. The River Ob can be seen as two meandering lines flowing from west to east across the centre of the image. The white lines are roads between oil production sites. The city of Surgit is just right of centre.

ST PETERSBURG

Here we see the city of St Petersburg in winter. The city is built on what used to be a swamp at the head of the Gulf of Finland. A storm surge barrier stretches from both sides of the gulf to the island of Kronstadt in the middle. The barrier protects the city from flooding by storms in the North Sea.

Russia and its neighbours

In the south, deciduous forests have been cleared for farming and further south, the flat, treeless grasslands of the Steppes have been ploughed up to grow crops such as wheat and barley. Much of Kazakhstan and Turkmenistan is desert with sand-dunes and palm trees. Only 10% of the land can be used to grow crops.

Collective farms

Under the communist government, land belonged to the state but peasants were allowed a small private plot of land to grow fruit and vegetables or rear a few animals. Villages were organized into huge collective or state farms. These farms were managed by a committee which received orders from planners in Moscow. The planners decided which crops to grow, what animals to keep and how much to produce.

The decline of communism

There have been some changes to this system. The big state farms are being broken up into smaller farms. Farmers can choose what to grow and where to sell it. But there is a shortage of modern equipment, such as tractors and chemicals such as fertilizers.

Food shortages

This system of farming has led to food shortages. In some places food is rationed, and there are long queues for basic necessities such as bread and milk. People with private plots use them to provide food for themselves. They sell any surplus in local markets.

New dams

During the 1960s, the planners in Moscow wanted to increase agricultural production so they built dams along the Syr Darya and Amu Darya rivers which drain into the Aral Sea. Water built up behind the dams and was used to generate hydro-electricity and to irrigate the land. Crops of cotton, grapes and citrus fruits were grown. These crops are valuable and many are exported.

The Aral Sea disaster

Water is removed from the rivers in such large amounts that the Aral Sea is now drying up. Chemicals used on the crops are washed into the rivers and flow down to the Aral Sea. Fish are dying from chemical poisoning and the increased saltiness of the water. The amount of water taken from the rivers must be reduced or the Aral Sea will dry up completely within the next 40 years.

▲ This fishing boat has been left high and dry by the shrinking of the Aral Sea. All over the area the former sea bed is now a sandy waste land.

◄ These men from Usbekistan have worked on cotton farms in the area all their lives. Cotton is the main crop grown on the irrigated land because it is very valuable. Locals call it 'white gold'.

ARAL SEA

Since 1960 the Aral Sea has shrunk by as much as 40%. It is now 435 km long and 290 km wide. It is nearly three times as salty as it was 30 years ago. This has caused the extinction of 20 species of fish. Many local fishermen have had to move away as the lake died and the fish disappeared.

This is an area on the Pacific coast in Russia where there are many active volcanoes and earthquakes. The volcanoes we see here are up to 5 000 metres high. They erupted in 1991, sending up a plume of ash and smoke.

India and its neighbours

India is the largest country of the region and has more than 750 million people. Every year, between May and November, rain-bearing **monsoon** winds blow from the south-west into India, Pakistan and the region. Farms depend on these rains. In some years the monsoons bring too much rain and vast areas are flooded. Precious farmland disappears beneath the water and crops and animals die. Other years the monsoon rains are poor and bring very little rain. This results in drought and the threat of famine as crops and animals die in the fields.

Water all year
Dams have been built across rivers such as the Indus in Pakistan and the Ganges in India to prevent this dependence on the monsoon.

▶ **This woman in Bangladesh is making a pot. Skills like these are passed from generation to generation and help people to be self sufficient.**

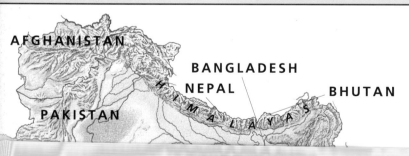

AFGHANISTAN

BANGLADESH

NEPAL

BHUTAN

PAKISTAN

HIMALAYAS

SRI LANKA

INDIAN OCEAN

This region has more than 1 billion people; 20% of the world's population. Most people live in the wetter coastal areas or on the fertile plains of the Indus and Ganges Rivers. More than 70% of the people are farmers, so there is intense pressure to produce as much food as possible from the land. Farms are small but India produces enough food for all its people.

The Himalayas stretch across Afghanistan, Nepal, Bhutan, northern India and Pakistan. They are covered by permanent snow and ice. The valleys of the Indus, Ganges and Brahmaputra support millions of farmers. The Ganges and Brahmaputra reach the sea at a huge delta which is Bangladesh. The Deccan Plateau covers southern India.

▼ **This is a view of the rooftops of the old city of Delhi. The city became India's capital in 1911. At the same time the foundation stone was laid south of here for the city of New Delhi which became the capital in 1931.**

Valuable crops
Water stored behind the dams is available to irrigate the land throughout the year. In other places wells have been sunk to reach water deep underground. Rice is one of the main crops grown on the irrigated land, as well as cotton, tobacco and other valuable products.

The hot sun
Some of the irrigation water is evaporated by the hot sun. As it evaporates, the water leaves salts near the soil surface. These salts can eventually kill crops planted there. The only way to get rid of them is to install expensive field drains and add even more water to

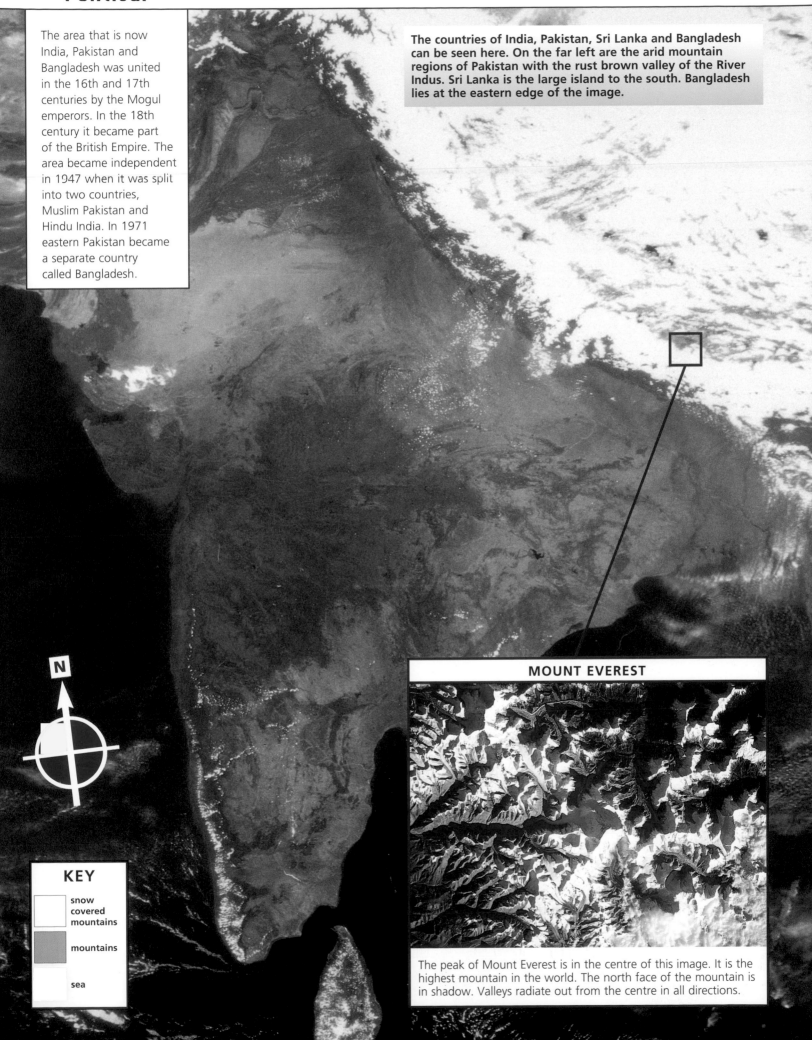

The area that is now India, Pakistan and Bangladesh was united in the 16th and 17th centuries by the Mogul emperors. In the 18th century it became part of the British Empire. The area became independent in 1947 when it was split into two countries, Muslim Pakistan and Hindu India. In 1971 eastern Pakistan became a separate country called Bangladesh.

The countries of India, Pakistan, Sri Lanka and Bangladesh can be seen here. On the far left are the arid mountain regions of Pakistan with the rust brown valley of the River Indus. Sri Lanka is the large island to the south. Bangladesh lies at the eastern edge of the image.

N

KEY

⬜	snow covered mountains
⬛	mountains
⬜	sea

MOUNT EVEREST

The peak of Mount Everest is in the centre of this image. It is the highest mountain in the world. The north face of the mountain is in shadow. Valleys radiate out from the centre in all directions.

India and its neighbours

India and Pakistan are two of the most industrialized countries in the region. Both have a long history of metal working and textile manufacture. Many of these traditional industries were wiped out when the British ruled the area. Since independence in 1947, some of these industries, such as making cheap, cool clothing, or producing gold and silver jewellery, have been revived.

Large-scale industry
The heavy industries such as iron, steel, chemicals and engineering have grown since 1947. India has deposits of coal and iron ore in the Damodar valley region and this area has become a centre of heavy industry. Pakistan's steel comes from Pipri near Karachi, where access to the port makes the coal and iron ore easy to import.

Nuclear power
Industries which use steel have grown in importance in the region, especially the manufacture of railway locomotives and cars in India. Pakistan has textile, food processing and chemical industries. Both countries have developed nuclear power stations to generate electricity and have branched out into lighter industries such as computer manufacture.

The flood problem
Bangladesh regularly suffers from devastating floods. The Ganges River and the Brahmaputra River meet here and reach the sea at the giant, low-lying Ganges delta. The two rivers begin in the mountains of Nepal. Heavy rains in Nepal create floods downstream where the rivers meet.

A giant sponge
In the past the trees covering the mountains in Nepal acted as a giant sponge and soaked up the rainfall. The rain was released gradually into the rivers and took longer to reach Bangladesh. This reduced flooding. Now many trees are cut down for firewood and to create farmland. People downriver suffer as a result.

Tidal waves
Typhoons in the Bay of Bengal sometimes create tidal waves which swamp large parts of the Ganges delta. More than 110 million people live in Bangladesh and many have been killed in the floods. Typhoon shelters have been built on stilts for people to use if they are warned in time.

▲ Floods in Bangladesh are common. Some are caused by rivers such as the Ganges and Brahmaputra overflowing their banks. Other floods are caused by typhoons. These typhoons create tidal waves that flood areas near the coast.

◄ These women are working on a building site in the state of Gujarat in India. They are carrying heavy loads of earth, bricks and cement as part of the construction of the

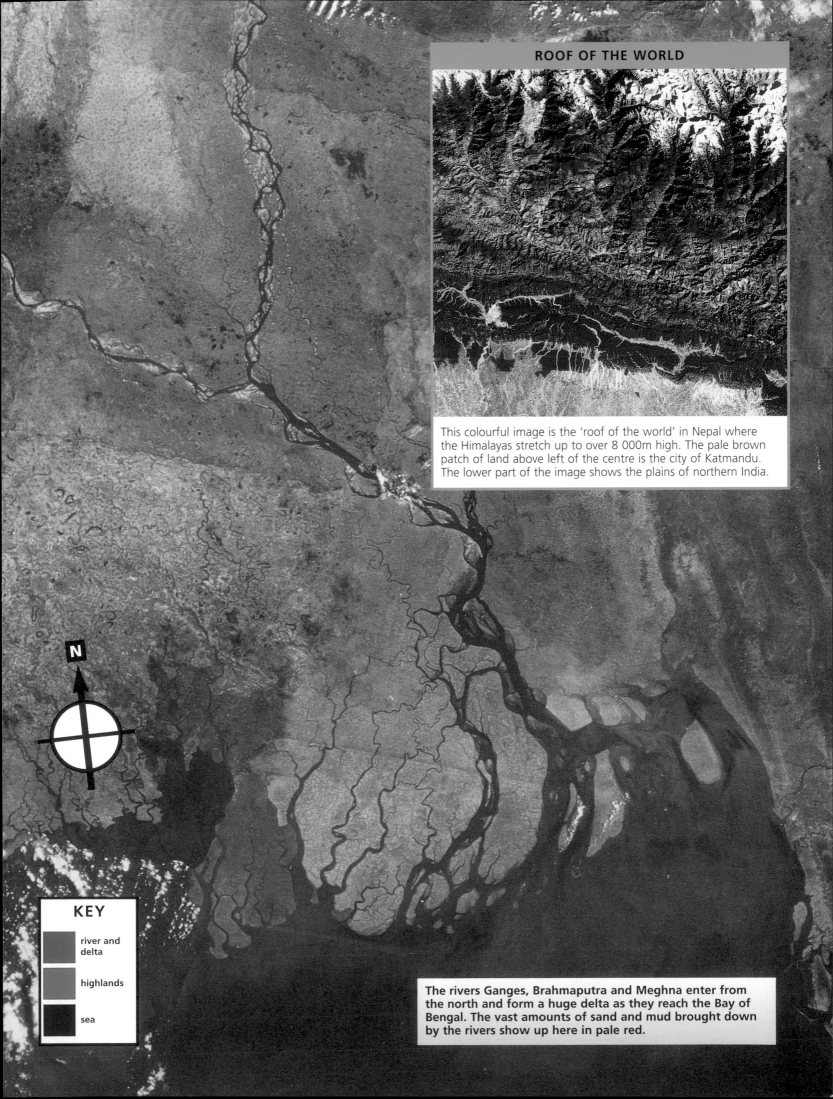

ROOF OF THE WORLD

This colourful image is the 'roof of the world' in Nepal where the Himalayas stretch up to over 8 000m high. The pale brown patch of land above left of the centre is the city of Katmandu. The lower part of the image shows the plains of northern India.

KEY

river and delta

highlands

sea

The rivers Ganges, Brahmaputra and Meghna enter from the north and form a huge delta as they reach the Bay of Bengal. The vast amounts of sand and mud brought down by the rivers show up here in pale red.

China and its neighbours

This area is one of the most densely populated parts of the world. About 1.1 billion people live in China alone. One in five people in the world lives in China. Every centimetre of farmland in China has been used to feed its people.

China is a country where the varied environment offers many challenges. Mountains called the Himalayas in the south and west of the region make communication and farming difficult. Further east the giant rivers Huang He and Chang Jiang often create problems by flooding.

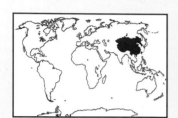

China dominates this region both in size (9.5 million sq km) and population (1.1 billion). Most people in China are farmers and their main diet is rice. Rice is grown in flooded fields in the southern and eastern parts of the country where the climate is wet and the soil is fertile. Land is owned by the village and people work on **collective farms** and share the harvest. In the north and east, the weather is drier and cooler and wheat and maize are grown. Land is scarce so hillsides are terraced to create flat land to grow food. Despite civil war, drought and floods, China has managed to feed its rapidly growing population. This is a major achievement.

Industrial development

Since 1949 China has developed its deposits of minerals such as coal, iron ore, oil and manganese. China now has iron, steel, engineering, chemical and textile industries. The country's progress has been so great that it now sends satellites into space. Despite this progress, many factories in China are still using old equipment and modernization has been gradual.

Industry outside China

Taiwan is a major producer of electrical and electronic goods from computers to television sets. South Korea, helped by massive American investment, has become one of the newly industrializing countries (NICs). South Korea exports ships, cars, computers and electronic goods all over the world. Hong Kong is a major centre for industry, banking and finance.

◄ **Rice is an important food crop in China. The seedlings have to be planted out in fields flooded by irrigation water. The broad brimmed hat gives the woman protection from the heat of the sun.**

▼ **These bicycles form a rush-hour traffic jam in Tiananmen Square in Beijing. Bicycles are a popular mode of transport because they are cheap.**

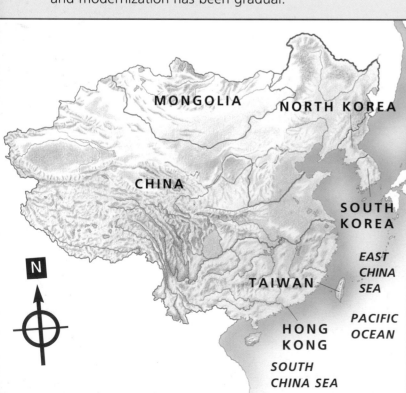

MONGOLIA

NORTH KOREA

CHINA

SOUTH KOREA

TAIWAN

EAST CHINA SEA

PACIFIC OCEAN

HONG KONG

SOUTH CHINA SEA

N

The growth of tourism

Tourism has become a growth industry in much of this region. At one time visitors were not welcome in China but now thousands of tourists visit sites such as the Great Wall of China, which was built 2 500 years ago and runs for 2 400 km. It is one of the few human features of the Earth which is visible from space.

Other tourist centres are Hong Kong, Taiwan, and China's capital, Beijing. Specialist tours visit the mountains of Tibet and its ancient capital, Lhasa, in the south-eastern part of China.

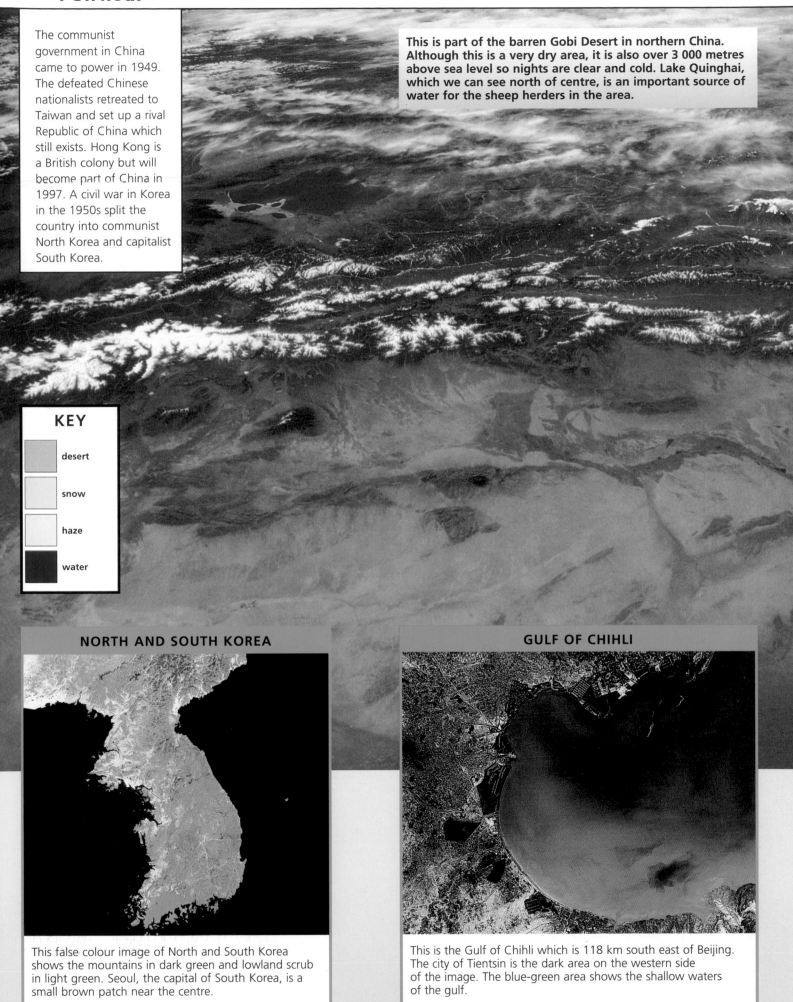

The communist government in China came to power in 1949. The defeated Chinese nationalists retreated to Taiwan and set up a rival Republic of China which still exists. Hong Kong is a British colony but will become part of China in 1997. A civil war in Korea in the 1950s split the country into communist North Korea and capitalist South Korea.

This is part of the barren Gobi Desert in northern China. Although this is a very dry area, it is also over 3 000 metres above sea level so nights are clear and cold. Lake Quinghai, which we can see north of centre, is an important source of water for the sheep herders in the area.

KEY

desert

snow

haze

water

NORTH AND SOUTH KOREA

This false colour image of North and South Korea shows the mountains in dark green and lowland scrub in light green. Seoul, the capital of South Korea, is a small brown patch near the centre.

GULF OF CHIHLI

This is the Gulf of Chihli which is 118 km south east of Beijing. The city of Tientsin is the dark area on the western side of the image. The blue-green area shows the shallow waters of the gulf.

Japan

Japan is a small, rich, crowded country where 125 million people live in an area of 337 683 sq km. This makes it a little larger than Britain, but smaller than California. Steep hills and forests cover 70% of Japan's islands and many rivers flow from the mountains down to the sea. Mount Fuji is the highest point at 3 776 metres and is permanently covered in snow.

Earthquakes and volcanoes

There are more than 50 active volcanoes in Japan and more than 1 500 earthquakes every year. Most quakes are so small that people do not notice them. The worst earthquake in 1923 destroyed most of the capital, Tokyo. New buildings have to meet strict regulations to ensure that they can withstand earthquakes.

Source of the sun

Japan is a long, narrow country. The north has cool summers and cold winters. The south has mild winters and hot, humid summers. The Japanese call their

There are 125 million people in Japan and they live on a series of small, mountainous islands. The lack of flat land means that towns and villages cluster at the foot of steep slopes. Forty years ago most people lived in small wooden houses with tiled roofs and rooms separated by paper screens. Today many city people live in modern, air-conditioned apartments.

Japan's air, land, water and wildlife have all suffered from pollution. Houses, factories and roads have eaten into the countryside. The air around cities has been tainted by smog from the fumes of cars, factories and power stations. Coastal waters were polluted by industrial waste. Now there are many restrictions on cars, factories and homes, so the air and water in Japan are becoming cleaner.

▲ **Fishermen at work on the island of Fukue. Japan has 430 000 fishing boats, which catch more than 13 million tonnes of fish each year.**

country Nippon or Nihon, which means source of the sun. The sun appears on their national flag. In autumn, parts of the country suffer high winds and heavy rain.

Fishing and farming

Farms cover only 15% of Japan's land because the mountain slopes are too steep to cultivate. Farms are small, but highly mechanized and use specially designed machines suitable for the tiny fields. Farmers use artificial fertilizers to produce high yields of rice, barley, wheat, beans, fruit and vegetables. Fish is the main source of animal protein. Japan is the world's leading fishing nation, and catches one-seventh of the world's fish.

Industrial success

Japan's wealth comes from its industries, which employ 34% of the workforce and account for 40% of the value of all goods and services produced there.

Japan has become one of the world's strongest economic and political powers. Its main trading partner is the USA. The Japanese invest in research and new products in order to remain successful. Japan has a key role to play as the Pacific rim becomes more important.

AKITA

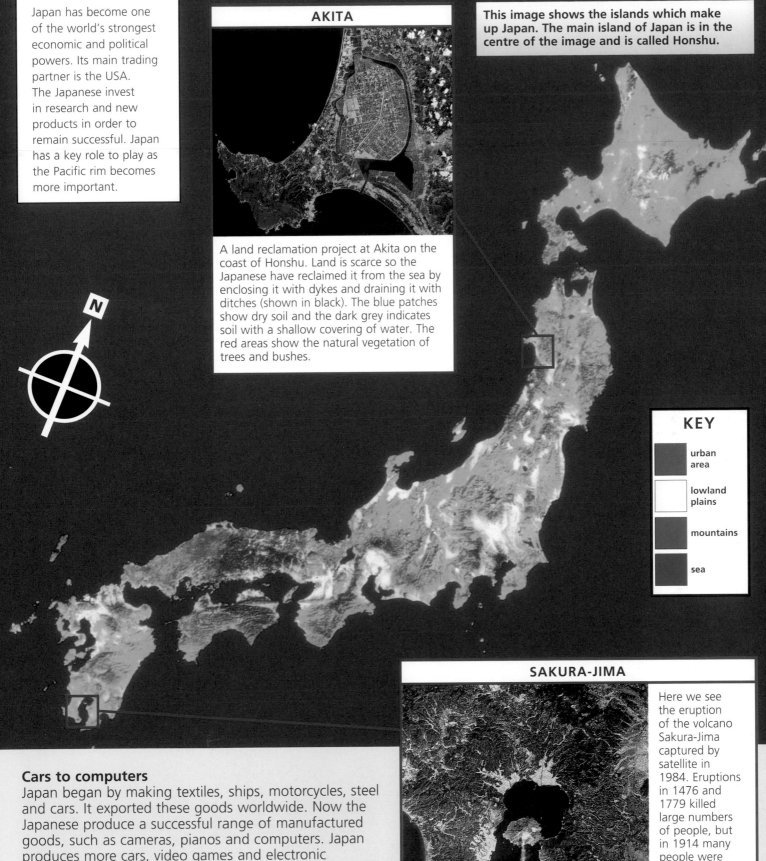

A land reclamation project at Akita on the coast of Honshu. Land is scarce so the Japanese have reclaimed it from the sea by enclosing it with dykes and draining it with ditches (shown in black). The blue patches show dry soil and the dark grey indicates soil with a shallow covering of water. The red areas show the natural vegetation of trees and bushes.

This image shows the islands which make up Japan. The main island of Japan is in the centre of the image and is called Honshu.

KEY

	urban area
	lowland plains
	mountains
	sea

SAKURA-JIMA

Here we see the eruption of the volcano Sakura-Jima captured by satellite in 1984. Eruptions in 1476 and 1779 killed large numbers of people, but in 1914 many people were saved by evacuation. The volcano has formed an island 10 km wide in Kagoshima Bay within the island of Kyushu.

Cars to computers

Japan began by making textiles, ships, motorcycles, steel and cars. It exported these goods worldwide. Now the Japanese produce a successful range of manufactured goods, such as cameras, pianos and computers. Japan produces more cars, video games and electronic equipment than any other country in the world.

The Japanese way

A Japanese company is like a family. Once people join they rarely leave. The company provides a home, schooling and medical services for employees and their families. Japanese workers rarely strike and have a reputation for hard work.

South-East Asia

More than 400 million people, or nearly 8% of the world's population live in south-east Asia. Cities are overcrowded and poor people live on the edge of urban areas in shanty towns. Outside the towns, people live on lowland areas near the coast or in river valleys. Farming is important everywhere especially rice-growing. Rice is the staple food.

South-east Asia stretches north and south of the Equator. Low-lying areas are hot and humid with an average temperature of 28°C. Upland areas are cooler. There is a long rainy season called the monsoon which drenches the area for weeks. These conditions are ideal for the huge tropical rain forests which cover much of the land.

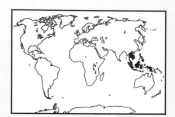

South-east Asia is made up of a narrow strip of mainland and thousands of islands. The country of Indonesia contains 13 000 islands and 177 million people. Most people in Indonesia live on the island of Java. South-east Asia as a whole occupies 5 million sq km of land, but spans 20 million sq km of sea – an area bigger than the USA.

Volcanoes and earthquakes
Many of the mountains and islands of south-east Asia are volcanoes. Earthquakes are common. The volcanoes are a mixed blessing. They bring very fertile soil but when they erupt they can cause great damage.

Threatened forests
The tropical rain forests which covered much of the region have been cut down for timber or to create farmland. Trees such as teak and mahogany are valuable exports. The sap from the bark of rubber trees is used to make latex which is needed to manufacture rubber. Malaysia, Indonesia and Thailand are the world's top rubber producers. Soil erosion has become a major problem in areas where the trees of the rain forest have been felled.

Oil in Indonesia
Oil was discovered in Indonesia and the wealth it created has helped the country to pay for imports of manufactured goods such as tractors. Indonesia is also using oil money to carry out a geological search for other minerals among its islands.

Developing industries
Singapore is a tiny island country but its position at the crossroads of air and sea routes in Asia has made it wealthy. A range of industries has grown up on the island, from shipbuilding to computers. Thailand and Malaysia are also developing industries. Malaysia has tin and rubber industries and now produces cars for export all over the world. Brunei is a tiny oil-rich country ruled by the Sultan who is trying to encourage industrial growth.

Varied languages
Many languages are used in south-east Asia. Malaysia has four official languages and the Philippines has 77 different languages spread across its 7 000 islands.

◄ **This woman is working in the Samsung electronics factory in South Korea.**

▲ **This picture shows the city of Singapore which is an oil refining centre and port. Its inhabitants enjoy the highest standard of living in Asia outside Japan and Brunei.**

From the 16th to the 19th centuries, the region was colonized by Europeans. There have been many wars this century between local people and the colonizing countries. Now the countries are all independent. In 1967, six of them: Indonesia, Thailand, Philippines, Malaysia, Singapore and Brunei formed ASEAN (Association of South-East Asian Nations) to increase wealth and trade between its members.

N

BANGKOK

This infra-red image shows the area around the city of Bangkok in Thailand. Bangkok can be seen on the right of the image. The pale areas near the sea are paddy fields with new rice plants. The dark red areas are rice fields ready for harvest.

This is a composite image of south-east Asia. The round-shaped area of land at the centre of the photograph is Thailand, Kampuchea, Laos and Vietnam. Malaysia is the long thin peninsula in the south west. Singapore is the city state at the southern tip of the peninsula.

Australia and New Zealand

Australia is a large landmass that covers 7.6 million sq km. The centre is a hot, dry area which has large deserts and huge sheep and cattle stations. A thin coastal plain lies in the east, near the Great Dividing Range of mountains. Most people live on south and east coasts where the climate is warm and wet.

The first inhabitants of Australia were Aborigines who arrived more than 40 000 years ago. Europeans did not arrive there until 200 years ago. Now 17.4 million people live in Australia. The first people to reach New Zealand were the Maori who came from Pacific islands such as Hawaii and settled there about AD 900. The first European to see New Zealand was Abel Tasman in 1642. British settlers came later.

More than 500 million years ago, Australia and New Zealand were joined to all the southern continents in one large landmass called Gondwana. Over millions of years, they drifted off into the Pacific. The plants and animals were isolated and evolved differently. This means that there are many plants, birds and animals in Australia and New Zealand that are found nowhere else in the world, such as the koala, the kiwi and the kangaroo.

The islands of New Zealand
New Zealand is cooler and wetter and lies 1 600 km south-east of Australia. It is made up of North Island and South Island. Most people live on North Island which has a mild climate.

City life
Most Australians live in towns and cities such as Sydney, Brisbane and Melbourne. Half of all New Zealanders live in the four largest towns of Auckland, Wellington, Christchurch and Hamilton.

Farming
Australia produces fruits, wines, wheat and wool. Areas near the rivers Murray and Darling have been irrigated to increase food production. New Zealand exports lamb meat and wool, timber and dairy products to the rest of the world.

▲ **Ayers Rock in the Northern Territory of Australia has mystical importance for the native Aborigines.**

▼ **Many parts of western and central Australia are hot and dry, so the main crop is grass. The grass provides food for huge herds of sheep.**

Industry and tourism
Gold, huge deposits of iron ore, bauxite, silver, lead and zinc have been mined in Australia. Steel, engineering, textile and chemical industries have developed on the east coast. Tourism is successful in Australia and New Zealand, and visitors flock to Australia's Great Barrier Reef and to New Zealand's volcanic springs, snow-capped mountains and deep fiords.

INDIAN OCEAN

CORAL SEA

NORTHERN TERRITORY

QUEENSLAND

AUSTRALIA

WESTERN AUSTRALIA

NEW SOUTH WALES

■ Sydney

VICTORIA

TASMAN SEA

PACIFIC OCEAN

NORTH ISLAND

TASMANIA

SOUTH ISLAND

NEW ZEALAND

N

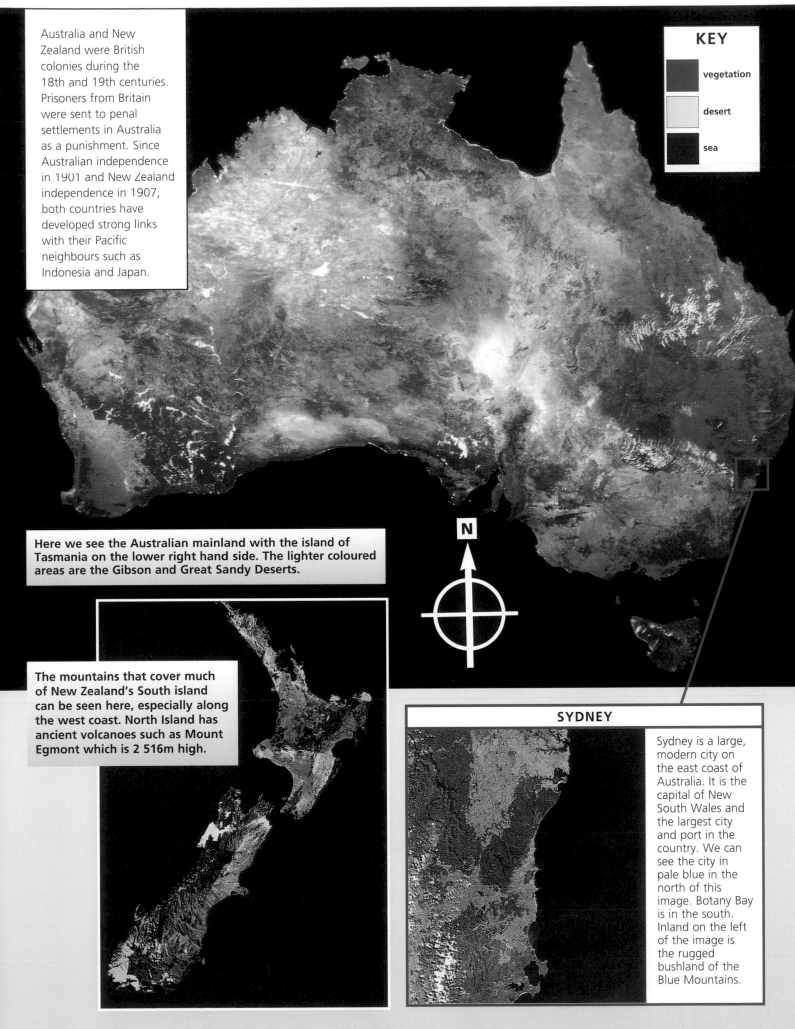

Australia and New Zealand were British colonies during the 18th and 19th centuries. Prisoners from Britain were sent to penal settlements in Australia as a punishment. Since Australian independence in 1901 and New Zealand independence in 1907, both countries have developed strong links with their Pacific neighbours such as Indonesia and Japan.

KEY

vegetation

desert

sea

Here we see the Australian mainland with the island of Tasmania on the lower right hand side. The lighter coloured areas are the Gibson and Great Sandy Deserts.

The mountains that cover much of New Zealand's South island can be seen here, especially along the west coast. North Island has ancient volcanoes such as Mount Egmont which is 2 516m high.

SYDNEY

Sydney is a large, modern city on the east coast of Australia. It is the capital of New South Wales and the largest city and port in the country. We can see the city in pale blue in the north of this image. Botany Bay is in the south. Inland on the left of the image is the rugged bushland of the Blue Mountains.

Pacific Islands

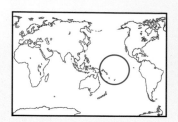

The Pacific is a vast source of fish. As the world population increases, the demand for fish goes up. But if fishing continues to increase, fish stocks will eventually dry up.

The people of the Pacific islands fall into three main groups. The Melanesian islands are closest to Australia and the people that live there are related to the Aborigines. The Polynesian islands are in the central Pacific and the first people here probably came from the direction of Asia. The Micronesian islands are in the western Pacific between the other two groups and are a mixture of the two peoples.

The thousands of islands dotted across the Pacific Ocean were formed in different ways. Some are the tops of mountains which rise steeply from the ocean bed. Other islands are formed from coral, a type of limestone rock made up of the skeletons of millions of tiny sea creatures called polyps. Some islands, such as Hawaii, are volcanoes where red hot lava creates huge clouds of steam where it meets the sea.

Controlled zones

The Law of the Sea Convention allows countries to create an exclusive economic zone (EEZ) for 200 miles around national shores. The countries can control fishing within these zones. The scattered islands of the South Pacific have created large controlled zones. Fishing fleets from Japan, Europe and the USA trawl for fish such as tuna within the zones, but refuse to pay duties for fishing there.

The ocean floor

The floor of the Pacific is a valuable resource. The sea bed has huge deposits of potato-shaped nodules which are rich in minerals such as manganese and copper. Deposits of minerals on land are running out so scientists are devising ways of removing these nodules from the ocean floor. Some Pacific countries are not wealthy enough to mine the sea bed and will need the help of richer nations such as Japan or the USA.

Tourism

Tourism is big business on many of the Pacific islands. Hawaii, Fiji and Tahiti are all popular destinations.

◄ **This girl is making a lei, a flower garland usually made from orchids which grow well on Pacific Islands. The leis are placed around the necks of visitors to the islands as a traditional greeting.**

▼ **Most Pacific islands have sandy beaches, behind which are steep mountains. The mountain slopes are covered with a dense green mat of vegetation.**

Tourism has paid for new roads, airports, hotels and restaurants. It has also brought changes to the island's traditional way of life and some locals resent this.

Small and large islands

Many of the smaller islands have few visitors and life there is simple. People live in small villages, grow food in gardens and fish from canoes. On the larger islands many people work in mines extracting copper or other minerals, or on banana, cocoa or orchid plantations.

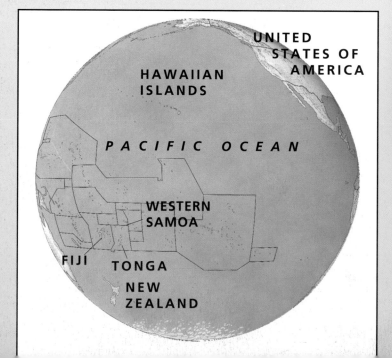

UNITED STATES OF AMERICA

HAWAIIAN ISLANDS

PACIFIC OCEAN

WESTERN SAMOA

FIJI   TONGA

NEW ZEALAND

The political structure of the Pacific islands varies enormously from island to island. Some are colonies of other countries. Others are independent and have their own governments. Many states share the common problems of being small islands in the midst of the vast Pacific. They often lack mineral or other resources and feel out of the mainstream of world politics. The Hawaiian islands form the fiftieth state of the USA.

DID YOU KNOW?

● The largest country in this region is Papua New Guinea which covers 1 385 000 sq km.

● The Pacific Ocean covers almost half the Earth's surface.

● The smallest country in the region is Nauru, and covers only 12 sq km.

HAWAII

We can see just how big the Pacific Ocean really is in this photograph. Australia and New Zealand can just be seen in the south west. The USA and Canada are in the north east.

This false-colour image shows the largest island in Hawaii, which is called Hawaii or the Big Island. This is a volcanic hot spot where lava comes to the surface. Old lava flows are shown in blue green from the volcano, Mauna Loa.

The Arctic

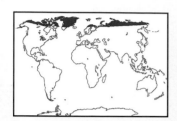

The Arctic has a harsh climate with long, cold winters and short, warm summers. For three months every winter the sun never rises. In summer the sun does not set for six to eight weeks.

Animal and plant life
Only 12 species of birds spend the winter in the Arctic, but in summer one-sixth of all the birds in the northern hemisphere arrive to breed. They have just a few weeks to hatch their eggs, then build up the reserves of fat that they need to fly south.

Survival strategies
Animals such as musk oxen survive by having long hair and a dense underfur. Polar bears are insulated from the cold by a thick layer of blubber. The transparent white hairs of the bears' coats attract the sun's rays to the back skin where heat is trapped by the bears' fur.

Ocean riches
A third of the Arctic Ocean is shallow offshore water around North America, Asia and Europe. These shallow waters are some of the world's richest fishing grounds. The sea provides food for marine mammals such as whales, seals and walrus. Every year 750 000 of them swim through the Bering Strait into the Arctic Ocean.

PACIFIC OCEAN

CANADA

SIBERIA

ARCTIC OCEAN

NORTH POLE

RUSSIA

GREENLAND

ATLANTIC OCEAN   ICELAND

Arctic people have suffered since the 16th and 17th centuries when Europeans arrived. Many Inuit (Eskimo) people died from diseases brought by outsiders. Illnesses such as measles proved fatal because they had no natural immunity. As outsiders rushed to develop oil and minerals in the region, traditional lifestyles in the area have been disrupted.

▼ **The Inuit now use modern technology such as this snow machine to travel in the fiercely cold environment.**

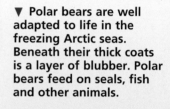

Unlike Antarctica, which is a continent surrounded by icy seas, the Arctic is an ocean hemmed in by North America, Asia and Europe. The southern limit of the region is the Arctic Circle. In 1989, the oil tanker *Exxon Valdez* ran aground and spilled 11 million gallons of crude oil in Prince William Sound. Pollution spread over 1 500 km of coastline. This was a warning that we need to protect one of the world's last great wilderness areas.

▼ **Polar bears are well adapted to life in the freezing Arctic seas. Beneath their thick coats is a layer of blubber. Polar bears feed on seals, fish and other animals.**

Mineral wealth
The Arctic area is rich in oil, natural gas, coal, iron ore, copper, lead, zinc, asbestos, gold and diamonds. In Alaska the discovery of oil at Prudhoe Bay led to a fight between environmentalists, oil companies and native peoples over the building of a 1 200 km long pipeline.

A permanent wilderness
In 1971 the native peoples were given 12% of the land in Alaska and $1 billion in cash. Pipeline construction began in 1975. In 1980, the US Congress declared 65 million hectares of Alaska a permanent wilderness. A new debate has begun on developing the oil found here.

From 1945 until the late 1980s, the former Soviet Union and the USA saw the Arctic as a potential battleground. The two superpowers built nuclear research stations and missile silos in Alaska and northern Russia. Relations between the countries have improved since the fall of communism in Russia in 1990.

GREENLAND

Greenland is a huge island surrounded by the Atlantic Ocean to the south and the Arctic Ocean to the north. Its coastline is cut into by many fiords. Almost all the people who live there live on the southern edges of the island in small villages where fishing is very important. Most of the island is covered by a huge ice sheet stretching into the distance.

The Arctic icecap is the white area at the centre of this image. The triangular spur pointing down from this is Greenland.

The Antarctic

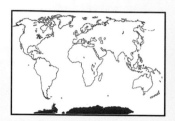

Antarctica was discovered in 1774 by the explorer James Cook. He saw the wall of ice and believed that land lay beyond. It was another 75 years before anyone set foot on the Antarctic.

Living resources
Antarctica's living resources are small. The largest land animal is a wingless midge about 1 cm long. There are only two flowering plants on the continent: the Antarctic hair grass and the Antarctic pearlwort. The rest of the vegetation is moss and lichen.

Plankton and krill
Although the land's living resources are poor, resources from the sea are rich. Plankton blooms and provides food for a shrimp-like creature called krill. The krill is food for whales, seals, fish, squid, penguins and birds.

Anti-freeze
Fish in this area are equipped with molecules of anti-freeze in their bodies to help survive the bitter cold. The Weddell seals live permanently under the ice in winter and use sonar to locate their food and find their way to breathing holes.

Antarctica has no **indigenous** population. Scientists are the only people who spend long periods of time on Antarctica, where they work in research stations. They study layers of ice millions of years old which show how the climate has changed and how pollution has increased.

Antarctica makes up 10% of the Earth's land surface. It is covered by ice up to 3 km thick in places. The ice holds 70% of the world's freshwater resources. Only 2% of Antarctica is ice-free. The rest is a giant ice cap. Ice cliffs and shelves stretch from the coast over the sea, breaking off into icebergs.

◀ These images show how scientists in Antarctica have discovered that the hole in the ozone layer is growing larger.

The top image shows high levels of ozone over Antarctica during September in the early 1990s.

The second image, taken a year later, shows how the ozone is becoming weaker.

▼ The British Antarctic Survey's research base is on the Brunt Ice Shelf at Halley Bay. Emperor penguins watch the unloading of the icebreaker *RRS Bransfield*.

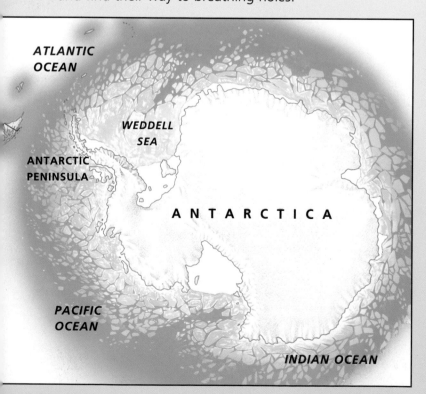

ATLANTIC OCEAN

WEDDELL SEA

ANTARCTIC PENINSULA

ANTARCTICA

PACIFIC OCEAN

INDIAN OCEAN

Living resources
In the past, Antarctica's living resources have suffered. Sealers almost destroyed the fur seals of the Southern Ocean. Whalers killed almost all of the region's blue whales, humpback whales and fin whales. Despite this, Japan, Norway and Iceland continue whaling.

Mineral resources
Huge deposits of coal, iron ore, lead, copper and uranium have been discovered in Antarctica as well as reserves of oil and gas. Pressure has now increased to develop the area's resources. Antarctica has been preserved so far, but, as the world's resources run out, attention will swing back there.

In 1959 the Antarctic Treaty was signed. This banned nuclear testing and waste disposal and allowed scientific investigation by all countries. In the 1980s, the Antarctic Treaty came under threat because of the area's mineral wealth. Antarctica is now a world park and development is banned.

ANTARCTICA

The colours in this image have been used to show the ice that covers most of the continent. The Ross Ice Shelf is the brown coloured area below centre and the Ronne Ice Shelf is the purple area left of centre. The Trans-antarctic Mountains form a line just below the centre.

The continent of Antarctica is the white land mass at the south of this image. Australia is at the centre, with New Zealand to the south east.

Glossary

Here are some simple explanations of the main terms used in this book.

atmosphere   The layer of air, containing gases such as water vapour and carbon dioxide, that surrounds the Earth. The atmosphere is a very thin layer around the Earth.

Aztec   An ancient tribe of people who ruled large parts of modern Mexico from the 14th century to the 16th century. Their capital Tenochtitlan was on the site of Mexico City.

carbon dioxide   A gas found in the atmosphere. When people breathe out they expel carbon dioxide. Plants absorb carbon dioxide and use it to build their cells.

collective farms   A type of farm found in many communist countries. These were large farms where the land, animals, machinery and equipment belonged to the state. As communism has declined, many collective farms have been broken up and the land leased or sold to the people.

contaminated   Polluted, spoiled or sullied land that has been exposed to radioactivity. This land is contaminated and takes a long time to recover.

desertification   This happens to an area when land dries out, vegetation dies and the area gradually becomes desert.

economic development   The development of agriculture and industry in an attempt to improve the quality of life of increasing numbers of people.

electromagnetic spectrum   The range of radiation produced by objects and measured and recorded by satellites.

equatorial   Areas close to the Equator which have a hot, wet climate for most of the year. Many equatorial areas are covered by thick forests.

geology   The study of the rocks which form the Earth's surface. Different rocks have different properties, for example some contain oil, others contain gold. Geologists search for valuable rocks.

Gulf Stream   A current of warm water which flows from the Caribbean across the Atlantic to Europe.

hydro-electric power   A way of generating electricity by using falling water. Most hydro-electric stations need to build dams and create reservoirs to store water. These reservoirs provide a regular supply of water for the hydro-electric power stations all year round.

indigenous   Belonging to a particular place or country. Indigenous energy supplies are the coal, oil and natural gas found in a particular country.

Industrial Revolution The introduction of modern industrial technology to production methods. It started in Britain in the 1760s when steam was used to power new machines.

intensive farming A type of farming which aims to get the maximum amount of crops or animals from a particular area of land. Intensive farming uses chemicals and machines.

Lapps A group of people who live in northern Norway and Sweden. They have herds of reindeer which supply them with meat and clothing.

mechanized Using a lot of modern machinery. Most agriculture in the UK and USA is highly mechanized and uses tractors and combine harvesters.

monsoon A climate in which the winds change direction as the seasons change. When the winds blow on to the land they bring heavy monsoon rains to Asia.

nomadic People who move from place to place herding their animals in search of water. These people have no permanent homes and carry all their possessions with them.

Pacific rim The countries around the Pacific such as the USA, Japan, Taiwan, South Korea, Colombia, Canada and Chile. Many of these countries have the fastest growing economies in the world.

radiation Energy given off by the Sun and reflected by objects on the Earth and in space. Radiation varies from high frequency, short wave-lengths to low frequency long wavelengths.

residential suburbs These are the parts of towns and cities where most people live. Suburbs are built away from the city centre and may have blocks of flats, houses or both.

shanty towns Areas of housing which grow up around the edge of cities in poor countries. Shanty towns have no proper water, sewage or electricity supplies and people build their houses out of discarded scrap materials.

terraced Steep hillsides are changed by building walls across the slopes and filling in the space behind the walls with soil. This creates areas of flat land called terraces. These small areas of land can then be used to grow crops.

tributaries The many small streams which join together to form a larger stream or river.

veneers Thin pieces of wood glued to the surface of poorer materials to create a higher quality and more expensive effect.

visible spectrum Those parts of the radiation spectrum which can be seen by the human eye.

This astonishing photograph offers an aerial view of the Karakorum Range in the north west of the Himalaya mountains. These glaciated peaks are up to 8 000m high.

Index

Numbers in **bold** indicate an illustration. Words in **bold** are in the glossary.